T0197179

SURVIVING A HOT MESS LIFE

And Overcoming the Neon Signs

FAITH HARRIS

WESTBOW
PRESS®
A DIVISION OF THOMAS NELSON
& ZONDERVAN

WestBow Press books may be ordered through booksellers or by contacting:

WestBow Press
A Division of Thomas Nelson & Zondervan
1663 Liberty Drive
Bloomington, IN 47403
www.westbowpress.com
1 (866) 928-1240

ISBN: 978-1-9736-6509-0 (sc)
ISBN: 978-1-9736-6508-3 (hc)
ISBN: 978-1-9736-6510-6 (e)

Library of Congress Control Number: 2019906981

Print information available on the last page.

WestBow Press rev. date: 10/10/2019

Dedication

Who doesn't cry or at least choke up after watching *It's A Wonderful Life*? I never let a Christmas season go by without watching that movie; however, unlike most people who cry at the end, I cry at the beginning. I know you are probably trying to think back to the beginning to figure out what would bring tears. It's the prayers, remember? The movie begins by hearing all the people in town praying for George. I have always felt that he was the luckiest man in the world. Can you imagine so many people loving you enough to bring your name before God's throne like that?

I have been blessed to have a group of people who have faithfully prayed for me on a regular basis for many years. When I have been at the end of my rope, not knowing how I would make ends meet, feeling rejected, believing myself to be a hot mess loser, these people have loyally come to my rescue. There have been times when I lay in my bed at night and imagined God hearing all those prayers being said simultaneously **for me**, just like the ones for George. I am overwhelmed and know I'm one of the luckiest people in the world!

I dedicate this writing to my husband, Neil. His love and support are heaven-sent. He looked past the hot mess years of my life, the mistakes I've made, and the scars that were left and has chosen to love me for the woman I am today. I also dedicate this book to some of my most devoted prayer warriors:

Ann, Jackie, Carol, and Nancy, my zany friends whom I have met with and prayed with every week since October 1996; my children Hope and Jasper, whose mere existence reminds me that I couldn't possibly be a loser because I have been blessed with two wonderful kids; my church family; my Emmaus family; my lifelong friend Amy, who was instrumental in my salvation and my connection to my husband, Neil; and all the other people who have come to my rescue when I felt the presence of a neon sign hanging over my head that read "Loser." They simply held a mirror up before me…one where the reflection was not that of a loser …but one where the reflection is a child of the King! My love and sincere thanks to all of you who allowed me to feel as lucky as George Bailey.

Contents

CHAPTER ONE
OBEDIENCE TRAINING

*But even more blessed are all who hear the
word of God and put it into practice.*
Luke 11:23 (NLT)

God prodded me to write this book for many, many years. During that time I came up with various reasons not to. First, I'm not a professional writer. I kept telling God that He was talking to the wrong person! After all, I've never had any formal training in writing other than my college composition class, which was a long time ago; therefore, I ignored God's request.

Besides, I didn't have time to write. I was working a full-time job and two part-time jobs, what you do when you are a single mom with two kids in college. I was also actively serving in my church and doing volunteer work. Just when was I supposed to find time to write a book? I kept telling God that He was going to have to show me how to squeeze this task into my already overloaded schedule. Be careful what you ask God to do because in response to my protest, I suddenly was downsized out of a job I had had for over seventeen years! Because I was blessed with a generous severance package, I didn't have to find a job right away and found myself with some spare time on my hands.

My next excuse was who would want to read something I wrote? Surely there were many more fascinating or well-known people God could use for this task, but He ended this argument by leading me to several stories in scripture. In Exodus 3 and 4 He chose Moses to lead the people out of Egypt, but when He told Moses what He wanted him to do, Moses argued that he wasn't a good speaker and was certainly not worthy. He said, "Please, Lord, send someone else" (Exodus 4:13 NIV). When Moses finally decided to be obedient to God, He was able to do great things through this man. I was also reminded that God used Mary and Joseph, two common people, to give birth to His one and only Son. Scripture teaches that God uses ordinary people, so the focus will be on Him and what He can do instead of being on the person He is using. All God was asking me to do was write my story...not save a nation, not birth a baby...just write.

Well, I had time to write, and I didn't have to be well known or eloquent, but I was very distracted at home. When I merely started thinking about writing, the phone rang, someone stopped by, or I would have a strong urge to stand in front of the open refrigerator looking for something to eat. After examining the fridge and the pantry, I would usually resort to calling a friend to see if she wanted to meet at a restaurant for lunch. It just seemed impossible to get any writing done. Of course, God wasn't going to let me get away with that excuse, either. When it was time for me to reserve the cabin that my children and I rented every summer in the north Georgia Mountains, as I was making reservations, the owner of the cabin asked what I was doing, and I proceeded to tell her that I had lost my job and for some unknown reason, included how God was pressing me to write a book (I had not shared this with even my closest friends). I was halfway expecting her to laugh, but instead she offered the cabin to me for a week, free of charge, so I could get away and write. I thought, *Okay, God, I hear You!*

One by one God kept knocking aside all my excuses. My last

protest was that I didn't actually know what to say in my book. I was reminded that when Jesus had directed Simon and his fellow fishermen to go back out into the lake and cast their nets after they had been out fishing all night and had caught nothing, they protested. Why should they waste more time by returning when there didn't seem to be any fish to catch? They didn't realize that it wasn't up to them to catch the fish. God just wanted them to be obedient and cast the nets, and He would take care of the rest. And when they did... "they caught such a large number of fish that their nets began to break" (Luke 5:6 NIV). I finally chose to be obedient to what God was asking me to do. I have cast my net and will leave the fish up to God.

What you are about to read is what God directed me to write. My prayer is that it will bless you and that you will walk away seeing yourself through God's eyes and not the eyes of the world.

This book is written for everyone who wants to be more...but thinks they are less.

CHAPTER TWO

CAN YOU HEAR ME NOW?

*You will seek Me and find Me when you
seek Me with all your heart.*
Jeremiah 29:13 (NIV)

Before I begin my story, you need to know that God talks to me. I know there are many people who don't believe that He really talks, but He does. People have asked me *how* He speaks to me. The truth is that God speaks in many ways.

I have struggled most of my life thinking that I had some sort of neon sign hanging over my head telling the world that I was a hot mess, a loser, and unworthy of being truly loved. This feeling was so overwhelming to me at one point that I ended up hibernating in my home. I had been a fairly outgoing person and had worked with youth groups at various churches for over twenty years; however, at that time in my life the feeling of shame and being a failure consumed me, leading me to take a sabbatical from youth work and just stay home. I felt that my ministry was pointless and devoid of making a positive impact in the lives of the youth. After all, what possible good was I doing working with kids when I felt like such a loser? The sad thing was that I *believed* that I was indeed a loser, and I was filled with self-doubt. I was in the midst of throwing myself one of the best pity parties of all time when the phone rang. It was Penny, a girl from my very first youth group, calling all the way from Germany! She said that God had laid my name on her heart and directed her to call me. Amazingly she felt the need to thank me for the positive influence I had been to her during a very formative time in her life when I was her youth director. In fact, because of the role model I had been, she was now working with youth herself.

A few days later I happened to run across a soldier who was stationed nearby. I was shocked when he called out my name because I hadn't recognized him. It was Roy, another youth from my very first group. He was excited to see me after many years and said he needed me to know what an impact I had on his life: I stood there astonished.

The next day at church a gentleman approached me to thank me for the work I had been doing with his grandson. In the past he had always had to drag the young man kicking and screaming to youth group; however, now that I was his youth leader, the grandson was reminding *him* that it was time to go to church.

God had been speaking to me through these other people and telling me that I hadn't wasted my time working with the teens. If I had made a difference in the lives of those kids, I must not be such a loser after all. God encouraged me personally and convinced me to continue in youth ministry. He speaks to us through other people.

For clarity's sake, let me say that I don't believe that there are *coincidences* in the life of a Christian. I call them *God-incidences* or *God-things* because when we give our lives and circumstances over to Jesus, He is in control; but I do believe that we can make choices that result in us snatching things from God's hands and putting them in our own. I understand that God was speaking to me through the circumstances of losing my job, getting a severance package, and then providing me a place to write. Some people will say that it was just a coincidence that the owner of the cabin offered me her place to use as a haven at the same time I was struggling with finding a place; but I know that this was God saying, "This is the time and the place." You see, not only was the cabin an ideal place for me to get away, but God also took me back up to the north Georgia mountains to the very town where I began attempting to fight the shameful loser mentality almost twenty-nine years earlier. The owner of the cabin didn't have any way of knowing about that. In fact, God had to remind me about it, too. God often speaks through circumstances.

Have you ever discovered a verse in the Bible that you had read or heard multiple times when suddenly the light comes on and it becomes very personal to you? The verse that God illuminated to me several years ago when I found myself shaken by divorce and wondering what was going to happen to me was Jeremiah 29:11 (NIV): "'For I know the plans I have for you,' declares the LORD, 'plans to prosper you and not to harm you, plans to give you hope and a future.'" These were the words of encouragement I needed to hear at the moment I needed to hear them. It has become my life verse, one that I recite over and over each time my world begins to look uncertain.

God kept using scripture to defeat my arguments about writing. I knew all those verses. I had heard them most of my life, but suddenly, just when I needed to hear the truth they held, God brought them back to me and spoke to me through His word.

It's easy to pick up a devotional book or other form of Christian literature that speaks to you and your need. In this day of the computer age, you can even have materials sent to an email inbox; however, did you realize that God could be the one leading you to select what would minister to your specific needs? He does this for me all the time. I know that some people say that it's just a coincidence when that happens, but you already know how I feel about those things. When I was struggling with the fact that God had asked me...an ordinary woman...to write this book, I just happened to pick up the book *Hugs from Heaven: The Christmas Story* by G. A. Myers and LeAnn Weiss while I was in Walmart one day. Flipping it open I turned to a page that said, "God entrusts extraordinary things to very ordinary people." It went on to tell how God used "Mary the poor virgin, Joseph the blue-collar carpenter, and shepherds baby-sitting smelly sheep in a field." Ah, yes, God indeed uses ordinary people...on purpose! This message was what I needed to hear at just the right time. You can think what you want, but I believe the timing for me to read those words was a God-incidence.

Often when we are totally focused on God during our own prayers, we will verbalize something that surprises even us. We ask ourselves, "Where did that idea come from?" I believe that God allows our deepest thoughts to come out of our mouths sometimes as truth pushes its way from our hearts up through our mouths, landing on our lips. There are other times that God speaks to us through the prayers of other people. As I struggled with God's call for me to write a book, I kept it to myself. I was too scared to tell other people what God was asking me to do. I was afraid they would laugh and ask, "Who do you think you are?" One Sunday morning during our ministry time at church, I asked one of the pastors to pray for me. When I approached him, he wanted to know if there was something specific I needed from prayer. I said, "No, I just want you to pray for me." As he began – with no direction from me – he prayed that I would realize that God was calling me to use the gifts He had given me and to expand my own personal ministry. He stated that God had been telling me for some time (How did he know that?). He continued by saying that God had taught me a lot as He brought me through my dark valleys and into my own healing, and it was now time for me to share my experience with others. There's no way that this pastor could have known any of this on his own. It had to be God directing his prayers in order to speak to me.

There have been times when I could honestly tell you that

God whispered in my ear. I could almost hear Him speak audibly because I felt such a strong sense of His presence; in addition, what He said to me was extremely profound. Years ago when I was crumbling inside from the intense pain of my failing marriage, one of the men I worked with invited me to visit his church. I thought it would be a nice change to go where nobody knew me or expected anything from me. I walked into that small congregation meeting in a school and sat down on the back row. I can't tell you much about what went on in that service, but I felt an overwhelming peace for the first time in years. In the midst of the sermon, I heard God whisper in my ear, "This is where you will stay until you are healed." I thought I would make only a few visits there; however, I now call it my church home, and God has blessed me in immeasurable ways through the people of this loving congregation.

Quite often God wakes me up in the middle of the night to talk to me. I asked one time why He had to do that, and He told me that this was the only time when my mouth was in neutral long enough for Him to get a word in edgewise. Now when I wake up in the early AM hours and can't go back to sleep, I say, "OK, God, what is it You want to tell me?" Most of the time He then guides my thoughts and reveals something to me. Other times He says nothing, so I use the time to tell Him how much I love Him and how thankful I am for all that He has done for me. He really is an awesome God, and he loves to reach out through the Holy Spirit.

I'm not sure I could ever list all the ways God speaks to me because they are limitless. The truth is that God can use anything and in any way He chooses. Years ago, He began to communicate to me in a rather bizarre way. When my husband and I first separated, I began noticing that many times when I looked at the clock it was 11:11, sometimes in the morning and sometimes at night. Now don't get me wrong, I looked at the clock at other times, too, but I thought it was strange how many times it happened to be exactly 11:11. During this same time the story of God raising Lazarus from the dead kept coming up, in Sunday school material, in a sermon at church, even in a sermon on the radio. Then one day I was riding through Atlanta, rounded a curve on I-75, and on a big electric billboard the words "The Lazarus Story" were illuminated in huge letters. I thought what God was trying to tell me was that if He could raise Lazarus from the dead, He could also heal my crumbling marriage. Unfortunately, that's not what happened.

It seemed like the harder I prayed for God to show me what to do, the more often the 11:11 showed up. I even saw it on my clock at work and then a few minutes later I'd see it on the computer (They obviously weren't synchronized). My daughter wrote me a check for something, and the check number was 1111. Someone that passed me in traffic had 1111 on their license plate. I was really bothered, so I decided to search the scriptures for every book that had an eleventh chapter and verse. When I got to the book of John, I stopped. Verse 11:11 of John (NLT) reads, 'Then He said, "Our friend Lazarus has fallen asleep, but now I will go and wake him up."' I thought the two had to be connected, but what was God trying to tell me?

In the middle of my search for meaning of this strange occurrence, our Praise Team was asked to lead the music for the Holy Spirit Conference at Epworth By the Sea in coastal Georgia. For years this retreat center had served as a place of refuge for me, somewhere I would go in order to get away by myself and spend time with God. It was no accident that I was there because the date was November 11. Yes, it was 11/11. I was thankful for an opportunity to have some quiet time where I could pray and seek God's face, asking Him to reveal to me what 11:11 was supposed to mean. What I believe God told me is that if He can raise Lazarus from the dead, He can do ANYTHING! The 11:11 reflects that He has the plans for my life all lined up and under control, just like the "1's" were all lined up and orderly. I just need to TRUST Him.

When I left home to go to the mountains to begin writing, I received a phone call from my then twenty-year-old son, who informed me that he was very sick with the flu. I knew this was probably an attack of Satan to keep me from what God had called me to achieve. I bowed my head and asked God what I should do. Should I return home to care for my son, or should I go ahead to the mountains as planned? In the midst of the prayer, my phone rang and my good friend Reba said not to worry, that she would take care of Jasper for me. I glanced up at the clock. It was 11:11. I smiled. God was still in control! The morning I began writing, I glanced at the clock, and it again was 11:11. I had turned on the radio moments before that, and it was set to a Christian radio station. Right after I noticed it was 11:11, the female disc jockey said, "Thanks for tuning in, my name is Lazarus." I laughed and got tears in my eyes at the same time. I wished I could hear the girl say her name again, but I realized that it didn't matter if that's what she really said. What mattered is that's what God wanted me to hear. He's still in charge and He's got my life all under control!

In his book *A Gentle Thunder*, Max Lucado wrote:

> "Once there was a man who dared God to speak: *Burn the bush like You did for Moses, God. And I will follow. Collapse the walls like You did for Joshua, God. And I will fight. Still the waves like You did on Galilee, God. And I will listen.*
>
> And so, the man sat by the bush, near a wall, close to the sea and waited for God to speak.
>
> And God heard the man, so God answered. He sent a fire, not for a bush, but for a church. He brought down a wall, not of brick, but of sin. He stilled a storm, not of the sea, but of a soul.

And God waited for the man to respond. And He waited...and waited.

But because the man was looking at bushes, not hearts, bricks and not lives, seas and not souls, he decided that God had done nothing.

Finally, he looked to God and asked, *Have You lost Your power?*

And God looked at him and said, *Have you lost your hearing?"*

Hearing from God requires *intentional* listening. It has been one of the most important things God has taught me, the art of purposefully looking for Him and listening to Him. To hear from God, we must be open to when and how He chooses to speak.

Fast Forward to 2019...

Most of this book was written in 2002 when there was life before texting, cell phone cameras, social media, and instant messaging. We had cell phones, but you paid for the minutes, especially for long distance calls. Most people had only desktop computers. There were a few (expensive) laptops, but hardly anyone had them. It was a time without iPads or iPods. You get it. We were on the cusp of the digital world, but we hadn't crossed over. We could send emails, but most of the time people had to wait until they got home to read them on their computers. The only thing you could do on a cell phone back then was talk. No texts. No emails.

Elsewhere in this work you will see "Fast Forward 2019" to bring you up to date on what has changed since the original manuscript was written seventeen years ago. Needless to say, because God has guided me through so much more since 2002, I must share all with you.

The term "hot mess" has become very trendy over the past several years. I feel like I was the poster child for this term even before it was a popular phrase. "Hot mess" can mean many things. Most people have their own definition, but the urban dictionary contains probably the closest definition to how the term is used today; A person (*usually female*) that is in an untidy or in a messy state, either emotionally or visually, but maintains an *attractive* look about her. Since I'm a combination of OCD and a perfectionist, my home and work areas are very organized. I always try to look put together on the outside, but inside is where my hot mess lives. For most of my life, my internal self has been one huge disorganized system of messy emotions. Can you relate? To be honest, there are still periods of time when God must step in and try to untangle the hot mess I have allowed myself and others to create. Thank God, He never gets tired of rescuing us!

CHAPTER THREE

WHERE IT ALL BEGAN

*"Do not be afraid of them, for I am with you
and will rescue you," declares the Lord.*
Jeremiah 1:8 (NIV)

"You were a mistake. You should never have been born!" These were the words spoken to me by my dad from the time I was a little girl. The wounds in my heart from the sting of his words were what I believe led me to my first feelings of being unloved and being a loser. During these early years the imaginary neon sign began flashing over my head. Shame controlled the *on* switch. I thought the whole world could read the sign. It said, "Loser!" and had an arrow that pointed down to me. Those feelings are something that have haunted me most of my life. Perhaps you or someone you love has felt these negative feelings at one time or another, too. If so, my story is for you. It's not fun to open up and bare your soul to other people, but I believe that's what God has asked me to do. When He first told me to write this book, I wasn't sure what He wanted me to say. Then He gave me the title. I pray that you will be able to use my words to find healing in your own life. When I finally opened myself up to God and asked that He heal me, He began speaking to me and teaching me in ways I never thought possible. Before going any further, please stop and ask God to speak to you through what you're about to read.

I don't believe my dad's intention was to hurt me like he did. He was adopted when he was six years old after living in an orphanage for several years. To my knowledge, he had no recollection of his real mother. All he knew was that in his mind she didn't want him, so she gave him up for adoption. He would always say, "My mother never loved me and neither do you." As I learned from the book *The Gift of the Blessing* by Gary Smalley and John Trent, my dad never received the gift of unconditional love. If you don't have something, it's hard to pass it on. Unfortunately, I didn't understand this idea until after I was an adult and my dad had passed away.

Mama was an only child. When she was ten years old, her mother suddenly passed away, forcing her to step up and be the "woman of the house." Her father was a prominent Miami architect who didn't have much time for a little girl and her needs. She met my dad when she was just seventeen and still in high school. He was in the Air Force and stationed near her home. They dated only briefly before eloping, infuriating her father. Mama was desperate to escape and thought marriage was the answer. A month after they wed, she became pregnant with my brother. Life was swiftly getting more difficult for her and my dad. To make matters worse, Mama became pregnant with me only four months after giving birth to my brother. My dad was so furious that he took her out on a dirt road and made her attempt to pick up the rear-end of the car in order to force a "natural" abortion. Perhaps my stubbornness began here. All their efforts to abort me failed, and I was born anyway.

Dad was unhappy with his life and began drinking more and more. The alcohol would completely consume him and always drag him into depression and the memory of his mother's rejection. As most alcoholics do, he had to find a target for his anger. He chose me. Even as I write these words so many years later, there is a deep sadness in my heart. Nothing I ever did seemed to please my father. I longed so much to crawl up in his lap and have him tell me that everything was going to be all right and that he loved me. But that didn't happen. The more he drank, the angrier he got. He would yell and tell me everything was my fault. If I hadn't been born, he wouldn't have to drink. He was very verbally and physically abusive. I believed the lie that everything was somehow my fault and that I deserved the abuse. The more he drank, the more devastating and bizarre the punishment. The beatings with the belt (that many times caused big welts and left blood bruises on me) would have been bad enough, but the punishment didn't stop there. If I spilled food on the floor at dinner, he would force me to get down on my hands and knees and lick it off the floor like an animal. One night I was washing dishes in the sink. He came from behind and shoved my face in the dishwater, holding my head down until I felt like I was going to pass out from holding my breath.

In an effort to find unconditional love, I poured my love into our family cat, Sparky. When dad really wanted to hurt me, he would bind Sparky's front paws with duct tape and make him hop around like a bunny. Then dad would jerk the tape off, stripping Sparky's legs of fur. I was forced to watch this torture; and if I said anything to him about it, he would punish me more.

At a young age I started becoming a perfectionist. I thought if I could do everything right, my dad would start to love me. It never happened. This treatment led me to live a life of low self-esteem, accepting blame for every bad thing, and of course, the feeling that the whole world believed I was a loser. This thinking had such a hold on me that when my grandfather suddenly died of a heart attack when I was only four, I thought that somehow I had caused it, a guilt I lived with for many years. I became a people pleaser. I had learned early in life that if I tried to defend myself when being punished, the punishment would become even more severe; therefore, at age eight when an older neighborhood boy held me down and forced me to have sex, I just lay there and took it. I thought to myself, "Just get it over with."

By the time I was a teenager, I was very unhappy, filled with shame, and the loser sign was blinking brightly in my mind. My parents were always fighting, and my dad's anger toward me had gotten more intense. My older brother "escaped" into his own world. He started hanging around with the wrong crowd, sneaking out of the house, drinking, and smoking pot. My mother was focused on trying to straighten him out, causing even more family dysfunction. My younger brother, who was four years younger than I, was the apple of my dad's eye and could do no wrong. I strived harder and harder to do everything right to avoid my dad's temper and punishments and to try to gain his affection, but I failed. I even made straight "A's" in school but when presented with the report cards, Dad would make fun of me to my brothers and say that I must have cheated.

My mother thought if we moved to another state we could leave my dad's drinking buddies and my brother's bad influences behind and our lives would improve. So when I was in the ninth grade, we moved to South Carolina. Of course, it wasn't long before my dad found new drinking buddies, and my brother fell in with another "wrong crowd."

I was miserable. I had left all my friends behind and had no way to get away from the abuse. When my mother couldn't stand the situation any longer, she took my younger brother and moved back to Atlanta, leaving me to take care of my dad and my older brother. I was devastated! At the age of fifteen, I attempted suicide by swallowing a bottle of aspirin. The only result was profuse vomiting. I decided not to admit to anyone what I had done because then they would really know what a loser I was; I couldn't even successfully kill myself! A few months later, my mother finally sent for my older brother and me, and I got to leave my dad behind.

Shortly after returning to Atlanta, I ran into Amy, a girl that I had gotten to know when we occasionally attended church. She invited me to go on a youth retreat with her the following weekend. I gladly went; I jumped at any opportunity to escape the tension at home. The youth director took us to a rustic campground in north Georgia. While there, we gathered in an outdoor tabernacle to have our worship service. I listened intently as the youth director explained how Jesus loved all of us. He even loved me! Unconditionally! He continued that there was nothing we had to do (or could do) to earn God's love. It was a *free gift*. We also couldn't do anything to make Him stop loving us. He went on to say that Jesus died and was nailed to the cross to prove His love for us. In fact, if I were the only one on earth, Jesus would have done it all just for ME! I had never known love like that existed. God was standing there with His arms out, ready to receive me, no strings attached. All I had to do was accept the gift that Jesus had died for my sins. So on a Saturday night in north Georgia, I knelt in front of an old rugged wooden cross and asked Jesus Christ to come into my heart and to be my Savior. For the first time in my life, I was filled with peace and hope.

Life began turning around for me. Not only did I become active in the youth group at my church, I became a leader. I was truly smiling for the first time. People noticed the change in me, too. For the time being, the neon sign had been turned off.

CHAPTER FOUR

HIGH MOUNTAINS AND DEEP VALLEYS

*This means that anyone who belongs to Christ has become
a new person. The old life is gone; a new life has begun!*
2 Corinthians 5:17 (NLT)

When I was sixteen, my parents decided to divorce. Within a year my mother remarried and moved about twenty miles away. My younger brother had gone to live with my dad, so my older brother and I lived together in the old family home. In order to make ends meet, we both had to go to work right away. Because I was still in high school, I had to work every day after school and on weekends. Attending church became a challenge; thus, my growth with the Lord slowed tremendously.

During this time I fell in love for the first time. This guy, who was two years older than I, was everything a girl could want. He was handsome, smart, polite, and he was a Christian. We dated throughout high school and had planned to get married. Even though we fooled around a little more than we should have, we never had sex. It was very important to both of us that we remain virgins. I had confided in Freddy about the sexual act that had been forced on me as a child, but he insisted that he didn't think it "counted against me." So as far as he was concerned, I was still pure.

Freddy knew about my family problems. He had even been there one night when my dad came over to bring my younger brother for a visit and got into a huge fight with my mother. It ended with my dad pinning my mother to the floor in a chokehold. I ran up and began hitting my dad and demanded that he let her go. He turned and said, "This is all your fault! We wouldn't have gotten a divorce if it hadn't been for you! You've ruined everything!" I was again filled with shame, and the neon sign turned back on. In my mind now even Freddy knew that I was nothing but a loser.

My friend Amy had decided to attend a small college in the north Georgia mountains where her sister had gone. Thank God I was awarded a sizable scholarship and with the help of grants was able to go with her. Next to my salvation, this was the most freeing experience I had ever encountered. The only person who knew me there was Amy, and I had done my best to keep the truth about my family from her. While at college, for the most part I separated myself from anyone else in my past, including Freddy. I wanted a chance to start over in a place where nobody knew anything about me.

College life was so much fun, and the peace I felt residing in the mountains was exhilarating. I felt as if I could breathe for the first time in my life. It was then that I fell in love with the beauty of the mountains. I could see God's handiwork all around me and felt His presence near. The loser sign disappeared, and I was once again at peace. God had given me the new beginning my heart had longed for.

I decided not to date for a while as I continued to sort out my feelings about Freddy. After a couple of months, though, a very attractive guy asked me out. He was considered one of the "studs" on campus, and of course I was extremely flattered that he asked *me* out. I was having a great time at the party he took me to until another friend informed me that my date had won a "prize" that night. He continued to explain that there was a bet made to see who could get me to go on a date, and the winner would win something like a six pack of beer. My self-esteem hit the floor. According to my friend the guy didn't really like me; I was just part of a stupid game. I was crushed! How could I have been foolish enough to think a popular guy would really be interested in me? Tears welled up in my eyes, and I asked to go back to the dorm. The next day the guy came and apologized, said he had a great time, and asked me out again. We dated for a couple of months until he decided that I was "the kind of girl that you want to marry," and he wasn't really looking for marriage at that time. So he dumped me. Even though I was hurt, I was proud of myself for sticking to my values and staying away from alcohol and sexual temptation; however, I ended up not dating for the rest of that school year. Every weekend I stood gazing out the window of my third-floor dorm room, watching the guys come pick up their dates. And again, I felt like a lonely loser.

During the summer after my first year of college, I took a job working as an entertainer and bird trainer at Kings Dominion Amusement Park near Richmond, Virginia. Yes, that's right, a bird trainer. I had worked the two prior summers at Lion Country Safari near my home in Atlanta, and now my former boss had moved to this theme park. We performed with the trained parrots, showing their tricks for the crowds. Doing these shows was always a blast, good money, and people were quite impressed with me. In fact, I was even offered my own local children's television show, much like Romper Room. No lit-up loser sign now! Unfortunately, I wanted to finish college, and the job would have required that I stay in Virginia. Even though I was extremely flattered, I turned the opportunity down.

A co-worker had pursued me the entire summer, but I wasn't

interested. The truth was I missed Freddy. He had called a few times, and we were to see each other again before returning to our respective colleges; however, the last time he called, he informed me that he had been dating someone else, and they had become quite serious. I was crushed. Two weeks before returning to college, feeling rejected, I told my coworker that I would go out with him.

Within the first hour of our date, he told me that he was thirty-one (I was nineteen). He drank a lot. I didn't. He told me that he had connections to the Mafia and that he had been married twice. I became very scared. What in the world was I doing out with this guy? He took me back home, which was the Days Inn Motel (since I was only living in Virginia for the summer), and he left.

The next night he returned. It was very late, and he was very drunk. The part of me who had learned how to take care of an alcoholic dad began taking over. I knew that he shouldn't drive, and so I stupidly offered him the other bed in my room to sleep it off. As you might have already guessed, he started making advances; and when I said "no," he lost his temper. The situation was all too familiar. When he began his attack, I tried to fight him off, but then the old mindset kicked in, and I became powerless. All I could say was "Just get it over with." Afterwards I sat on the bathroom floor crying. All that was important to me was taken that night. I felt ashamed and ruined.

CHAPTER FIVE

Making Bad Decisions

Be careful - watch out for attacks from Satan, your
great enemy. He prowls around like a hungry, roaring
lion, looking for some victim to tear apart.
1 Peter 5:8 (TLB)

Once again I decided to keep what had happened a secret. I thought if I just buried it down deep inside, nobody would ever know. I also decided not to bother to see Freddy again since I was "damaged goods" now, and I knew Freddy would never accept the fact that I was no longer pure. So, I packed my bags and returned to college. I was broken and a loser.

At the end of my freshman year, I had received the great honor of being asked to represent one of the fraternities on campus. Shortly after returning from our summer break, I began dating one of the members. Because he was one of the leaders, I was thrilled that he asked me out, especially since I had such a low opinion of myself. As our relationship began to get more serious, I thought I needed to confess to him what had happened. At first he took my news pretty well. Shortly thereafter he began pressuring me to have sex because I was no longer a virgin. One night I finally gave in and said to myself, "Just get it over with."

Boy, had I messed up my life now! I was totally disgusted with myself. When he decided he wanted to marry me, I jumped at the chance. Besides, who else would ever want to marry a hot mess like me? It didn't matter that I didn't really love him. I thought I could make it work out and my emotions would follow. What a bad decision!

We got married the next summer. Almost immediately the abuse began, both emotionally and physically. He said I caused it, and I accepted the blame. After all, this behavior was what I was used to receiving from the men in my life. I tried to get him to attend church with me, but he refused, saying he was ashamed of me. He somehow had decided that the sexual attack that prior summer was not a forced situation and began calling me vulgar names. His physical tirades became so bad that I was forced to wear long sleeves in the summer to hide the bruises. I never knew what was going to set him off, so I felt like I was walking around a ticking time bomb all the time. Sometimes it took me longer at the grocery store than he thought it should; and when I returned home, he would accuse me of having an affair, go into a rage, call me names, hit me, knock me to the floor and kick me, and sometimes he would throw objects at me. At one point he even picked up a wooden rocking chair and hit me with it, breaking the arm on the chair.

He would scream at me and repeatedly tell me how ugly I was, which I began to believe even though I had been a model in high school. The reflection I saw in the mirror was one of a loser, an ugly loser. There were times when I threatened to leave him, but he would laugh and ask, "Where do you think you're going to go? Nobody is ever going to love someone like you!" So when anyone called and asked how married life was, I would lie and say that it was great. As a child I had learned to put a smile on my face and pretend that everything was just fine. I was much too ashamed to admit the truth to anyone. After all, according to what I had been told by my father and now my husband, I deserved the treatment. I sincerely bought the lie that every bad thing was caused by something I had done.

Again, I shoved the pain and shame down in the depths of my heart and accepted full responsibility for all the things that had gone wrong in my life. The abusive pattern that began with my father was once again repeating itself in my life: extreme rage, physical beatings, being blamed for everything, and me accepting the guilt. I was convinced that these were the consequences of being a loser.

About a year after we were married, my husband came after me with a butcher knife, held it to my throat, and said he was going to kill me. Somehow I got away and made it to my car. As I pulled away, he yanked the passenger door open and bent the hinge, but I still managed to escape. I knew that I could no longer stay in the marriage but struggled with the thought that if I divorced him, everyone would somehow blame me. I finally decided it was a chance I had to take.

I moved away again, starting over in a town where nobody knew me. I was so angry with God. Was His love all a lie, too? If He really did love me, how could He allow all these horrible things to keep happening? No, I hadn't read my Bible in a long time. No, I hadn't done anything to grow in my relationship with Him. But where had *He* been when all of this was happening? I stopped caring about what God thought of me. I was a loser, and I didn't care what anybody thought about me anymore. I began dating guys who were also losers. Who cared? For some reason I had enough concern about myself not to sleep with them, but I began drinking. A lot.

One weekend a friend from work convinced me to go to Florida with her to have some fun in the sun. We took my VW Beetle that still had the passenger door tied shut (from my ex-husband bending the hinges). We didn't want to look "uncool," so instead of Rhonda getting in each time and sliding over (like we were on a date), she would take the keys, get in the driver's seat as if she were going to drive and then announce, "Oh, I don't feel like driving. You drive." Then I would go around to the driver's side, she would slide over. With a good excuse. And we'd be on our way. Two cool chicks.

I had always heard about girls meeting guys at the beach but had never experienced it until that weekend. While spending the day playing on the beach, we met two cute guys. After several hours of conversation, they invited us to dinner that night, and we gladly accepted, especially since we had limited funds. At the end of the dinner, Rhonda left with her guy to go for a walk on the beach. The guy I was with decided to drive me down the road to show me the hotels that had been destroyed by an earlier hurricane. I didn't have much choice because Rhonda had my car keys with her due to our little game of "I don't feel like driving." I knew it wasn't the smart thing to do because both of us had been drinking, but I went anyway. We got to the deserted area next to one of the partially destroyed, abandoned hotels. The next thing I knew, the guy was all over me. I told him to stop, but he said, "You didn't really think dinner was free, did you?" I began screaming, crying, and fighting him, but there was no one nearby to hear. Thank God I had an outfit on that had to be unzipped, untied, and unbuttoned in order to get it off. Before the guy succeeded, he reached his sexual release and sat back up. He then drove me back to my hotel and threw me out of the car. Rhonda was already in the room, so I was able to get in quickly. I jumped into the shower, clothes and all, and sat on the floor sobbing hysterically, trying to wash all the filth off me. The loser sign was now brighter than ever.

A few months later my stomach was eaten up with ulcers. I was one big hot mess! One night I threw myself down in a heap on the floor and cried uncontrollably for hours. I begged God to love me again. I begged for His forgiveness. I pleaded with Him to give me another new beginning. I was so tired of being a loser! I begged God to please turn off that neon sign that I felt was a constant daily reminder of what a mess I was. I committed to Him that I would do my part to clean up my act; then I fell asleep.

When I awoke the next morning, I felt much better. I met up with some friends I knew from the apartments I lived in and asked if they'd be interested in going to church with me on Sunday. They agreed. So for a few months the three of us went to church every Sunday, alternating between the Methodist and the Baptist churches. I was once again happy, peaceful and content!

A few months after we were regularly attending church together, I started having feelings for the guy in our little group. We began dating, and five months later we were married. It was so wonderful to be with a Christian. He also knew all the bad stuff from my past and loved me anyway. What a great feeling to be loved again! We joined the local Methodist church; and after the pastor found out I had been a leader in my youth group, he asked me to help him start a group for our church's teens. God's goodness was so overwhelming to me! I was filled with gratitude! And the best thing was that there was no longer an imaginary neon sign over my head telling me that I was a loser. Hallelujah!

After being married for only five months, I found out that I was pregnant with our daughter. Even though she wasn't planned, I knew she was a gift from God. My wonderful little family was coming together. I was so blessed! She was definitely the delight of my life!

Soon after I gave birth to Hope, fatigue began to plague me. Not only was I working a full-time job at the hospital and adjusting to being a new mommy, I was also trying to maintain the position of youth director of a rapidly growing group at church. We started with seven active teens, and the group grew to over fifty the first year. I was trying my best to be all things to all people, but I was failing. Most of the time I ended up feeling once again like one big miserable hot mess!

During this time my husband began feeling slighted by me. I just didn't have the energy to give him the degree of attention he felt he needed. The result was that he turned to another woman for his fulfillment. When I discovered his affair, all the negative feelings about myself returned. Of course, he defended himself by saying that his infidelity was my fault (which I accepted because I had always been told I was the cause of all bad things). The imaginary neon sign was back on.

Divorce was not an option for me. Not only did I not want to be single again, I believed that God wanted us to stay together. Besides, in my mind only a real loser gets divorced twice before she even turns twenty-five!

As we were trying to sort things out in our marriage, we suddenly discovered that my husband had testicular cancer. It had been misdiagnosed for a year, so by the time it was caught, it had spread into his lymph system. He also had a massive tumor in his back region. The doctors gave him a 50/50 chance of making it through the next six months. I begged God to spare his life. I also prayed that God would take some of the pain and sickness away from my husband; and if someone had to have it, He should give the pain and sickness to me. Lo and behold, prayer works! My husband would take the doses of chemotherapy, and I would go in the bathroom and throw up. He never got sick at any time even though he was taking extremely high experimental doses of chemotherapy, but I certainly did.

We finally got to go home from the hospital the week before Christmas, and I scheduled a visit with my own doctor. I was hoping he could give me something for the nausea and vomiting. Instead, he decided to run some tests on me. On Christmas Eve the phone rang. It was the nurse from my doctor's office. She asked, "Are you sitting down?" My heart sank. What was she going to tell me? Was I sick, too? She continued, "Congratulations! You're going to have a baby!" I was stunned. The doctors had told us it would be impossible for my husband to father another child. But

God gave us another miracle! After two surgeries and six months of chemotherapy, my husband was healed. And nine months to the day of the diagnosis, our son was born. What a wonderful gift from God! He wasn't even supposed to be conceived, yet there he was. My husband and I both rededicated ourselves to God, each other, and our family. It was time to move on. I believed then that the neon sign was gone for good.

CHAPTER SIX

SPIRALING DOWNWARD

*We are pressed on every side by troubles, but not crushed
and broken. We are perplexed because we don't know why
things happen as they do, but we don't give up and quit. ⁹
We are hunted down, but God never abandons us. We get
knocked down, but we get up again and keep going.*
2 Corinthians 4:8-9 (TLB)

The next eleven years went bumping along. We were the perfect little family...the one everyone wanted to copy. We were all active in our church, our community, and schools. Everything was as close to perfect as anyone could want. We did have an occasional roller coaster ride in our relationship, but upon asking my friends, this was to be expected. In many ways our marriage seemed a lot better than the rest of my friends', so I was filled with contentment.

Then my world fell apart. During a revival my husband felt convicted to admit to me that he had indeed had another affair. The news paralyzed me. I was speechless. My only response was to say that I forgave him. After all, I must have done something to cause this infidelity, too. I felt like a failure as a wife.

I quickly tried to bury this pain in my heart, but it was so full of all the other pain and shame that I had stuffed there through the years that I just simply couldn't hide one more thing. I tried my best to deal with the situation on my own because, of course, I could never admit to anyone that I was such a bad wife that my husband had to turn to another woman (again). If people found out, I was afraid they would somehow think less of me.

I spent the next few years wearing a plastered smile on my face so everyone would be convinced that I was happy. I thought that my theme song should be "Oh Yes, I'm the Great Pretender" because I had turned into a world-class actress. Not even my closest friends knew we were having problems at home, but my heart was heavy with the pain it harbored. When it appeared to me that my husband was having another questionable relationship with a third woman, I confronted him. He explosively denied everything, but my heart just couldn't trust him. His behavior and attitude had followed the same pattern of the previous two affairs. I tried to talk to him about the situation, but he became extremely angry and said that I caused the affairs. Our intimate relationship was haunted by the thought of him being with the other women. Every time we had sex, I ended up crying. I would always wonder if he was thinking about the others, wishing he were with one of them instead of me. I decided it was time to separate, so for the next year we slept in different rooms while I attempted to sort out my feelings of rejection and figure out what I had done to cause the situation.

As if the problems at home weren't enough, a situation at my job began to evolve and slowly became one of the biggest nightmares of my life. There was a very well-respected man at work who had become a good friend to my family and me. Our boys played sports together, and we even went to the same church for a while. When the situation at home began to get worse, my coworker caught me crying in my office one day and began to inquire. Desperate to talk to someone, I began confiding in him. Out of the blue one day, he marched in my office and said, "We need to have an affair." I thought it was a joke at first, but then realizing that he was serious, I began to tell him that it was out of the question. Unexpectedly he became extremely angry with me. When I refused to go along with him and did what I could to distance myself from him, he began behaving inappropriately when nobody else was around. He threatened that if I ever told anyone about what he was doing, he would deny everything, and it would be his word against mine. I accepted that everyone would believe him. After all, he was a respected business leader and was thought to be a strong Christian family man. On the other hand, I was under the impression that other people looked at me and saw my neon signs. I kept my mouth shut. Due to the deteriorating condition of my marriage, I didn't even feel that I could tell my husband. All the old memories from my past flooded my mind, paralyzing me and preventing me from protecting myself. When I purposely avoided the man or didn't act friendly to him in front of our coworkers, he would call me into his office and display a fit of rage. Again I felt powerless, so when he would start his sexual exploitation, I would say to myself, "Just get it over with."

I tried everything I could think of to make him stop. I even took a self-defense class to learn how to protect myself, but he found out and would always say, "You don't think you're strong enough to get away from me, do you?" Then when we were in front of other coworkers, he would make me show everyone what I had learned in class (even though I protested). Unfortunately, he had done such an excellent mental brainwashing on me, I was unable to break his grip. He proved his point.

Not only did he constantly tell me that he would deny everything if I ever told anyone what he was doing, but he also attempted to put my job in jeopardy. I began secretly looking for another job to escape the nightmare, but at the time the opportunities were limited. Occasionally my children would be dropped off at my office after school. Several times, he would put his arm around my daughter and say, "Look who I have." I was terrified that he would hurt her if I attempted to expose what he was doing, so I continued to keep my mouth shut and put up with the abuse. Because I had learned how to be the "Great Pretender" through the previous abuses in my life, absolutely nobody had a clue about what was happening.

In my attempt to cope on my own and to keep the rest of the world from finding out, I became physically ill. In fact, for almost a year I was in a doctor's office almost every month. The doctors had determined that my immune system was shutting down. The stress was taking its toll. Up to this point, I rarely ever shed a tear. Oh, I could cry for someone else or for people on TV, but other than a few select times, I never cried for me. Now I couldn't stop crying. I began to withdraw from my friends and became a hermit in my home. I hated going to work and dealing with my coworker, and I hated going home and dealing with my husband's anger. Part of me wanted to die. I even prayed that God would go ahead and take me off this earth. How messed up is that?

In what I believe now to be a God-thing, I found out that I was not the only female at work that was being harassed by this man. When I realized that there were at least four others and they were all willing to testify against him, I made a desperate call to turn him in and put a stop to the nightmare. Everything was to be handled quietly. Even though he was forced to leave the company, he told his family and a few coworkers that *I* was the one who had come on to *him*, just like he threatened to do. And, of course, the rumor spread. He mentioned no other woman's name, just mine. We had all received a settlement from the company in exchange for our silence, so even if I had the emotional strength to "fight" him by pressing charges, none of the other women could come to my defense because of the signed agreement. I was mortified! He had made good on his threat, and other people believed him!

Our company decided to pay for counseling for all the victims. It was the best thing that could have happened to me. On my first visit I gave the counselor an outline of my "loser" life and cried, "Please help me. I don't want to be a victim anymore!" Over the next two years I would pour out all the pain, shame, feelings of unworthiness, and vile thoughts that I had harbored in my heart. At the same time my husband and I tried marriage counseling, but that ended after seeing a third counselor. According to my husband, there was something wrong with all of them.

After almost a year, with no change in our turbulent relationship, I took the kids and moved out. I also decided to visit a new church, one where nobody knew me and where I no longer had to pretend that I was living the perfect life. It became my safe harbor, the place where I felt God pull me up in His lap, wrap His strong loving arms around me, and whisper, "Everything's going to be all right."

A year later my daughter confided in me that my husband had tried to convince her and my son that I was having a nervous breakdown. He also told them (and other friends from church) that I wasn't even a Christian and asked them to pray for me. My spirit was so crushed! How could he tell people something like that, especially our children? By that time I had done all I knew to do to save the marriage, and since it only seemed to be getting worse, I filed for divorce. Yes, the neon sign started flashing again. I was ashamed that I couldn't make my marriage work. I pleaded with God to change me, change my husband, or change both of us. Nothing was different. I reminded God that I knew He had the power to do anything. At the time I thought perhaps we would go through the divorce and then get back together again. You know, like God raising Lazarus from the dead; however, I found out just a month after we legally separated that my husband already had a new girlfriend, whom he had been dating for some time. Later when they wed, I accepted that this "Lazarus" would be remaining in the grave.

Fast Forward 2019...

My sexual harassment situation happened twenty-three years ago. Last year women across the world began standing up against these types of workplace occurrences, called the "Me, too" movement. Men in very prominent positions were exposed, fired, and sued for the same type of behavior that I endured. Oh, how I wish this movement had been around when I was going through so much! The sad thing is that I have heard people making excuses for this horrible male behavior, somehow blaming the women. This attitude is wrong on so many levels. It's too late for me to do anything about my situation, but I'm thankful that other women are now courageous enough to speak up and stop inappropriate sexual talk and behavior in the workplace.

CHAPTER SEVEN

Putting it to the Test

*For I am convinced that neither death nor life, neither
angels nor demons, neither the present nor the future,
nor any powers, neither height nor depth, nor anything
else in all creation will be able to separate us from
the love of God that is in Christ Jesus our Lord.*
Romans 8:38-39 (NIV)

After I finished writing this part of the book in 2002, I did nothing with it for a little over a year. I convinced myself that God had encouraged me to write it for my eyes only as a way of healing me and moving me forward. And yep, that's what I did. Nothing. But then God, in His infinite ways, started telling me that I was supposed to share it with others to help them see that they aren't alone and to help them heal, too. I had this overwhelming sense from God that if I was obedient and released the book, "something BIG" was going to happen in my life. I finally decided to begin the process by letting my children read it. They were both in college by this time, so I thought they needed to know "who" I was, and they also needed to give me their permission to share it with others because it involved intimate information about their parents. To my surprise, they both encouraged me to share it with others. In fact, with my permission my daughter started sharing it immediately with some of her friends.

Every June our church holds its annual children's camp where we spend a week at a rustic campground in the country. I took the book with me and asked the pastors to read it and give me their honest feedback; they also were very encouraging. To me that still didn't mean I needed to publish it, just share it in manuscript form, which I, somewhat reluctantly, was willing to do.

The week after camp I was contacted by an old "friend" through Classmates.com. He was more of an acquaintance than a friend. We went to college together, but he was one of the leaders on campus; and because I was shy, we never had much of a real conversation at school. He was president of the student body, in the men's honor society, and performed around campus, singing and accompanying himself on the guitar. He had always been a big deal. Since graduation I had seen him only a couple of times at alumni events, where we shared some small talk, nothing more. Now here he was emailing me. I thought to myself, "This is the BIG thing God was talking about." I was excited. At the time I had been divorced for nearly seven years, and I was ready for a new relationship.

We did a lot of emailing and talking by phone since we lived about four hours away from each other. He would send me between five and ten questions a day to find out what I liked, what my favorite things were, and so on. After I sent him my answers, he would send me his answers to those questions, and then send more questions. We were learning so much about each other, and I was amazed how much we had in common. I shared all of this with the Fab Four (Ann, Carol, Jackie and Nancy: my four prayer partners), and they agreed that he sounded like he was perfect for me, although they did have some reservations about his past. The first time I planned to see him in person, I commented to the girls that if he was in any way as cute as he was in college, I was going to be in trouble because I was already having strong feelings for him.

The day we met, I was staying at a hotel in the town where he lived. I was there with a bunch of people from church who had also traveled there for a friend's wedding, so I felt safe. When I opened the door to my hotel room, there were a dozen beautiful red roses sitting on the desk. I was very surprised that he had gone to the trouble to do something so thoughtful. I remember him driving up, and I absolutely thought my heart was going to burst through my chest because I was so nervous! He stepped out of the car, and though we had both aged, he was still very handsome. I had decided to stand across the parking lot at another friend's room so I could see what he looked like before having to greet him. When he got to my door and started knocking, I came up behind him and said hello. He turned around, grabbed and kissed me, and that was all it took for me to be completely head over heels.

Jack had been honest with me; he had dealt with alcohol and prescription drug addictions, even doing some substantial jail time when he was caught with a forged prescription for pain medications. He also confessed that he'd been married five times. I had known about the first two wives because one was a sorority sister of mine from college, and the other had come with him to one of our class reunions. Needless to say, I was surprised and concerned about the other ones. Jack convinced me that the other three wives didn't count because he was only married to them for a couple of weeks each, and when he "sobered up," he always got an annulment. He had been clean and sober this time for over three and a half years and begged for me to see "the man he was today and not the boy he was yesterday." He told me that he was currently the director of a halfway house for men dealing with addiction recovery, "paying back to society for everything he had done."

He also talked about the wonderful healing ministry we would have together. Although it wasn't the ideal marriage situation for me and anyone else would have turned around and left, my compassionate, forgiving side that really wanted to be actively involved with this type of ministry decided to trust this man that I had fallen in love with. In addition, I prayed to God all the time to reveal if Jack was being dishonest with me or if I should walk away, but I didn't see any reason not to move forward. I earnestly thought this was God's calling for my life.

We decided to marry on New Year's Eve, five short months after we reconnected. The week before, on Christmas Day, I met his sisters and their husbands. They weren't extremely warm to me, but they were friendly. One of them took me to the side and asked if I knew about Jack's past. I assured her that I did, and not wanting to talk about it on Christmas Day, I changed the subject. None of them wanted to come to the wedding, which didn't seem to bother Jack, so I refused to be bothered either.

My mother had met Jack at Thanksgiving. She was very critical and said he was just "after my money, my house, and my health insurance." I was so angry with her for not supporting me that I told her not to come to the wedding. In fact, she and I barely talked during that period. She always thought I should marry a doctor or a lawyer (someone with money), so she was definitely not happy with Jack.

The wedding was beautiful and romantic. My girlfriends twisted my arm about having a formal wedding. I didn't think I should because of my past, but they convinced me to have a beautiful church wedding surrounded by hundreds of my friends and my children. They helped me with all the details, and it ended up being perfect! Of course, I had to pay for everything because Jack didn't make much money in his job. He had moved to my town the first of December and worked for only a few weeks in a temporary job. One of my friends who worked in mental health care had hired him, but that job didn't begin until after the first of the year. Another friend offered me her family's cabin in Gatlinburg, Tennessee for the honeymoon. So off we went on our way to live happily ever after. Or so I thought.

On the honeymoon Jack started feeling bad. He had told me that he had a kidney disease that caused him to have frequent kidney stones, and he'd even had several episodes during the five months that we had been getting to know each other and dating. It got so bad on the honeymoon that I finally had to take him to the ER. I told the doctor that he couldn't have pain medication because of his addiction history, but the doctor said, "Lady, nobody can go through this kind of pain without pain meds!" I had no choice but to allow them to administer the drugs. I just prayed against the addictions coming back to haunt him. And me.

When we got back home, Jack started his new job, and everything was wonderful! He joined the praise team at our church, so he again was playing and singing, some of the things that had attracted me to him in the first place. I was so proud of him! Friends were constantly talking about how happy I was; and they were right. But then everything started unraveling. Jack had a lot of accidents: his knee went out on him, causing him to fall and whack his face on the refrigerator, cracking his cheek bone and causing prolonged double vision; he then started having chest pains, and I had to call 911 because he thought he was having a heart attack. That ended with him having a heart stent inserted; a month or so later I had to call 911 yet again because he thought once more he was having a heart attack; he had more kidney stones; he tore his rotator cuff; he had to have two root canals; he got strep throat and on and on. On top of that, his mother was on her death bed, and every weekend we traveled to be with her and his sisters. Jack didn't want to stay with his sister who lived there, so we had to get a hotel room each time. As his mother got worse, we had to take additional days off from work to be with her. Jack lost his job from being out of work so often, and he wasn't eligible for unemployment.

He cried and said how sorry he was and that he had let me down, and he begged me to forgive him. He promised that he would find another job as soon as possible. In the meantime I paid for everything. I was working my full-time job and a part-time job trying my best to make ends meet. Even with that, debt began to pile up quickly.

I was worried about the mountain of medical bills and hotel and restaurant costs associated with his mother's illness and death as well as the entire wardrobe that Jack had purchased so that he would "look more professional;" however, I knew that I should get about $5,000 back on taxes, so that money would help. Normally, when you do your taxes online, you get the refund back in just a few weeks, but mine didn't come. I waited another few weeks and there was still no deposit in my account, so I finally called the IRS. They told me they had kept my refund to apply to Jack's back child support, which I knew nothing about. Before we married, I asked him point blank about his debt, and he told me he had NONE. Well, about a month after we were married, he started getting bills from various counties in Georgia where he owed fines. If he didn't pay those, they could arrest him since repayment was part of his probation, another situation that he had failed to mention. These fines amounted to nearly $10,000! In addition, a few weeks before we married, Jack's old car broke down and couldn't be repaired, so I had to buy another car. Luckily a friend was selling his daughter's car, and he sold it to me for a low price. I saw my happy little world once again crumbling around me; moreover, Jack was getting pain meds with every trip to the ER or doctor's office, and he couldn't find another job.

I was determined to make this marriage work. I thought with all that I had experienced, with my strength of character and the depth of my faith, I was strong enough to pull Jack through. I also got our pastors, the Fab Four, and other Christian friends to pray with me for Jack's healing and for him to find a job. I believe in the power of prayer. I've seen prayer work repeatedly. I know people who have overcome all sorts of trials and addictions, so I just put all I had into praying my way through this horrible situation; it was just another hurdle in my life. I had gotten through everything in my past with God's help, so I knew He could come to my rescue again.

In the middle of all of this, the president of the college we graduated from came to our town for an alumni event. When he found out that I was working for another university, he asked me to consider coming to work for my alma mater. Jack really wanted me to take the job, but it was in a rural mountain area and would be more challenging for him to find a job. He kept telling me that it was our chance for a clean start, a new beginning, and we would be right there in my "happy place." Therefore, we made a deal. At the first of June, I took the job but told the university I couldn't start until the end of August. In the meantime Jack would look for a job there, too, and if he couldn't find one, I would decline the position. I thought it was going to be next to impossible for him to find a good job, so we decided not to tell any of our friends.

Jack was gone most of that summer, staying at an inexpensive place he found, while he was job hunting. When I was about three weeks from my start date, he came home very excited because he had gotten a wonderful job that was only about a mile from the college where I'd be working. We were thrilled, and we finally told our friends that we were moving. I put my house up for sale, resigned from my job, and we moved to "God's country." Since my house didn't sell right away, the college rented us a small campus home that was usually available only to faculty. We expected to be in it for about three months until the house sold, so everything looked promising.

We settled in to our new town and our new home in the mountains. It was a dream come true...until... the Friday before Jack was to start his new job. He called me at work to say that his job offer had fallen through. We were both devastated! Jack cried because he had let me down again. He promised that he'd find another job, "even if it is just working at McDonalds!" I said, "OK." What else could I do? My house sold about a month later, so that gave us a nice financial cushion. And I prayed and prayed and got other people to pray that Jack would find another job quickly.

I went to work and came home each day and Jack was sitting there watching TV and hadn't done anything all day. My patience was wearing thin. We had friends who would come see us on the weekends, and, of course, Jack forbid me from telling anyone that he didn't have a job. He would always pick up the check for everyone if we ate out (paying for it with my money) and acted as though we had no financial problems at all. I was wearing a fake smile and pretending that everything was great, just like I had as a child and earlier in my adult life. But I continued to throw myself down at the foot of the cross and beg God for help.

In April the IRS kept my refund check again. I kept finding videos, CDs, and clothing that Jack continued to buy with my money. We had huge arguments. I was finally forced to take a loan out against my 401K to cover our mounting debt, including many more medical bills. By this time all the money I had made from the equity in my house had also been depleted. Jack had one "job offer" after another that was going to be great, but then each fell through at the last minute. We would fight, and he would cry and tell me that his parents never believed in him and neither did I. Sound familiar? It was the same type of emotional blackmail that my dad had used. I was fed up and determined not to be victimized by the triggers he was trying to pull. It was definitely not a happy time, but I was still going to be strong and faithful enough to make it all work.

Finally the middle of May he got a fabulous job working with a psychologist in a town about forty-five minutes away. He would again work with clients who were recovering from addictions. Not only was I happy that he now had a job, I thought working in this environment would help him with his own addictions. Jack got up every day and went to work. He was like a new man. He'd call several times a day with detailed descriptions about what he was doing, and he was always excited. Finally! I was doing many happy dances and praising God continually! And I could not wait until those paychecks started coming in! But he was only going to be paid once a month, so I had to wait a little while. I felt like the elephant that had been living on my chest had finally moved on. The release from the stress was unbelievable!

Jack always insisted on getting the mail out of our post office box, and I let him. After all, I couldn't care less about it. But one beautiful afternoon, a friend at work asked me if I wanted to walk to the post office with her. I said, "Sure!" I was excited to get out of the office and get a breath of fresh air. I grabbed my post office box key to see if any mail had come in since Jack picked it up on his way to work. I opened the box and was surprised to find it full. As I pulled the envelopes out, I realized they were bills from various ERs in different cities and states. I quickly stuffed them all inside a magazine that was also in there, said nothing about it to my coworker, and returned to my office. Later that afternoon, I told my boss I wasn't feeling well and went home.

As soon as I got away from campus, I called Jack. He answered in his usual happy little voice, but that ended quickly when I said, "You need to get your boss to help you get into a treatment center!" I proceeded to tell him that I had found the bills and knew he had a more severe problem than I had suspected. He hung up on me. I cried. I was so angry and disappointed! Hours went by, and there was no word from him. Around midnight I called him again but got his voicemail, so I left a message asking him to call me. We had to get him into treatment as soon as possible. He didn't call back. I was up all night, but he never called and never came home. I was filled with all kinds of emotion. I was upset at myself for thinking I was ever strong enough or had enough faith to make him change. I was mad at God for not answering my prayers for Jack's healing and freedom from the addictions. I was embarrassed about what my friends and family were going to think. I just didn't know what to do next.

When morning came, I called a friend who worked with the FBI. I told her the story about what had happened and asked if there was any way she could help me. She said she would call me right back. In less than five minutes, she did, telling me that she had called the place where Jack worked to see if he had shown up for work that day, but they had never heard of him! WHAT? I didn't believe her. She must have called the wrong place. So I called. She was right; they had never heard of him. He had made the whole thing up! I was furious and mortified! I started calling the other places where he had supposedly had job offers (that allegedly fell through for one reason or another), but nobody recognized his name! He had pulled a huge con job on me. He didn't even try to find a job. I called his sisters to tell them what had happened. I called the Fab Four, my children, and finally my mother. I knew she would say, "I told you so," which I deserved because she had been exactly right. For the next several days I kept calling Jack's cell phone until his mailbox was full and wouldn't record anymore messages. I had to call in sick that week. I couldn't possibly face anyone. I hadn't eaten. I hadn't slept. I just sat on the couch day and night hysterically crying and calling out to God.

And God spoke to me. I asked God why He let this happen to me. He reminded me that when I prayed and asked Him to show me if Jack was wrong for me, back when we were dating, He allowed me to see that Jack was going to the ER for kidney stones, his knee injury, his heart, and so on. I said, "God, those things could have happened to anyone." God then reminded me that I confronted Jack when I (through a gut feeling) discovered that he had gone to several pharmacies for pain meds that he hadn't told me about. We were only two weeks away from the wedding; and when I consulted the pastor, he advised me to postpone the wedding; but I thought I knew better. I believed I was a tough lady who could overcome anything. Besides, I didn't want to be alone anymore, so I ignored the warnings and moved forward. I had prayed, and God HAD answered. I just didn't listen. When we want something badly enough, we justify circumstances to get what we want. In this case I was starved for love. I had the love of family and friends, but I wanted romantic love with all the benefits. If I had held to my belief that a couple should date at least a year, through all the seasons and holidays, I most likely would have seen Jack for who he really was. A con man. But nooooo, I thought I could control the situation.

As I sat in my house all alone, Satan came to visit with the flashing loser sign again. I told him to get out of my face! He told me that everyone was going to say, "Now you (loser) have been married and divorced three times. You married this man so you could have romantic love, but that stopped two months after you got married (when Jack started having heart problems), and now what do you have? You have nothing but another strike against you!" I pulled out Bible verses that I had written down. They reminded me about how God sees me. And I shouted at the top of my voice, "Get behind me, Satan, I'm covered by the blood of Jesus!"

Jack didn't come home...ever. I returned to work and mentioned very little to coworkers; however, on a small campus word traveled quickly. The campus police even came to see me. They were worried that Jack would be dangerous if he came back on campus, and they insisted that I change the locks on my house. I was in a big war with Satan. He kept throwing shame at me, but I kept reminding myself about God's love and redeeming grace. Every day the mailbox was full of bills from before Jack disappeared. I got a large calendar and started plotting out the ER bills to see where he had gone every day while I worked. Because of our location, Jack was able to get to hospitals in South Carolina, Alabama, Tennessee, North Carolina and many cities in Georgia without me knowing where he was on any given day.

He had visited about two ERs a day, and I never knew anything. The bills amounted to well over $200,000! On top of that, he had gotten hold of one of my credit cards that I thought had a zero balance and had run that way up, too. Because I never got the mail, he was able to do many things without my knowledge. One of the Fab Four called an attorney friend from home who contacted me and said, "You have got to file for divorce as soon as possible so you aren't responsible for all those medical bills." You may be amazed to hear that I struggled with this idea. I didn't want that third divorce! I kept thinking that something else would happen to fix this horrendous mess, but time was of the essence, so I finally gave in and agreed to file. In addition to other debt we had on another credit card, I had to default on the loan against my 401K because I had no way to repay it; but at least I was not responsible for the bulk of the medical bills.

A month after he disappeared, I received a phone call at work. It was Jack. He had checked himself into a detox center. I called some friends who lived near there and let them know. They went over to see him; he had been living out of his car the whole time, and they helped him get into a rehab center he chose in South Georgia. At least that's what we thought was happening. As it turned out, he left there and moved in with another lady, shortly before he disappeared again. Luckily, I was able to serve him with the divorce papers, get his signature, and file for divorce before he disappeared that time.

It has now been over thirteen years, and Jack's three sweet sisters and I have continued to stay in touch. He has surfaced a few times in and around Atlanta but then always disappears again. I occasionally still get random medical bills that somehow find their way to me. At least those tell us where he's been and that, as of the date on the bills, he was still alive. Knowing even that small bit of information gives his sisters some form of comfort.

As for me, I am doing well. God rescued me financially when my grandfather passed away. He left my brothers and me some farmland in Illinois, which we were able to sell. I got just enough money to pay off the credit card debts. I moved back down to southeast Georgia and reunited with the Fab Four the year after Jack disappeared. I did have wounds, but once again, they don't own me. I hate like everything to have to admit my past to people; but as horrible as it all seems when it's written on paper, I have also been able to use my experience for ministry. Every once in a great while, the loser sign will try to flash, but I immediately remember that I AM A CHILD OF GOD AND HE LOVES ME VERY MUCH, I quickly tighten the lid on the garbage can that holds those neon signs.

In my life I have learned about dealing with people with addictions, first with my dad and then with Jack. I thought that if I had enough faith. If I prayed hard enough. If I had a deep abundant strength of character. If I gathered enough prayer partners to pray for Dad's/Jack's freedom from addiction, they would be set free. Satan could not beat me down this time because God taught me throughout my life that I can't control other people. Dad's and Jack's addictions and behaviors had nothing to do with me. They weren't my battle. I didn't cause them to drink or abuse prescription medications, and I couldn't cure either one of them. The only thing I, or you, can control is how much we will allow other people's behavior to impact us. Addicts must be the ones to choose recovery for themselves; until that happens, we are powerless to help them.

Does that mean we should look the other way and ignore the signs that they are drinking or using drugs? Not at all. We can offer emotional and prayer support, but we absolutely have no control beyond that. I do recommend counseling and/or a Christian support group like Celebrate Recovery. There are thousands upon thousands of people dealing with loved ones with addictions in all corners of the world. These groups can help you set up boundaries for yourself and for your addicted loved one. You don't have to go through the battle alone.

CHAPTER EIGHT

OH, TO BE ADORED

My grace is sufficient for you, for my power is made perfect in weakness. Therefore, I will boast all the more gladly about my weaknesses, so that Christ's power may rest on me.
2 Corinthians 12:9 (NIV)

Every little girl grows up dreaming that someday she will find her Prince Charming and the two of them will live happily ever after. Needless to say, by this time in my life that dream had been shattered several times, and I thought I might never experience love again. All I ever wanted was to be married to one man (and only one) and to grow old with that same man. We would raise children together and spoil grandchildren together. I wanted the "happily ever after" like a Hallmark movie, but so far that hadn't happened for me.

After being single and alone for six and a half years (since Jack disappeared), my girlfriends convinced me to try online dating. I had several friends who had met their husbands online, so I finally decided to bite the bullet. I signed up for the minimum amount of time because I was still quite skeptical; however, I must admit that reading the bios was quite entertaining. Some were hilarious! I never knew there were so many middle-aged men who liked to ride motorcycles and take long walks on the beach. I met a couple of guys who were *not* keepers, but I kept looking. I shared the bios of the men I thought were the most interesting with a few of my friends. My friend Ann kept saying, "Date the teacher." The teacher lived two and a half hours away from me, and I thought he would never be able to understand my crazy work schedule, which required a lot of nights and weekend work. After Jack disappeared, though, Ann was the one who told me that my "picker was broken" and from now on the Fab Four got to pick men for me. I never forgot that, so I decided to take her advice and communicate with the teacher.

His name was Adam, and he was a high school history teacher, former football coach, and athletic director. He was also a city councilman, so I figured a background check had already been done on him (After what I had been through, I wanted to make sure he wasn't another con man). We emailed for a couple of weeks, and then he asked me for my phone number. We had only short conversations, exchanged texts, and finally decided to meet. I wanted to arrange for a short visit in case it didn't turn out well, so we decided to meet at a restaurant halfway between his house and mine. I told my daughter and the Fab Four about the arrangement, and they were waiting to hear back from me. When I drove up to the restaurant, Adam got out of his truck. He was a big guy, 6'4" tall, overweight, but he had a sincere smile. After we ordered, we began to relax and talk. In fact, we talked for two hours until we were the only ones in the restaurant. It was a beautiful day, so we decided to continue the conversation outside, away from the ears of all the waiters who kept circling around us. Adam asked if I would be comfortable with us sitting in his truck with the windows rolled down. I had become very comfortable by this time, and because it was a very large truck, there would be ample room between us. He kept commenting on how nervous he was, which he said was very unusual for him. I, on the other hand, was very relaxed, probably because I had already determined that I wouldn't be seeing him again after this day. After all, he was very GU (geographically undesirable) because of the distance between us. Even so, my calmness surprised me because I had never felt that relaxed on a "first date."

After another half hour my phone started blowing up with phone calls and texts. I laughed and explained that the Fab Four and my daughter were worried that something had happened to me since it had now been over two and a half hours. He patiently waited while I responded and let them know that I was still there and everything was fine. The texts repeated every hour; and before we knew it, we had been talking for five hours! Finally, we decided that we better go home because both of us had quite a drive to return to our respective towns. I hugged him goodbye and really thought that would be the last time I saw him. As soon as I got on the interstate, I started calling the girls back. With each one I'd say that I thought Adam was "absolutely precious," seemed to be a man of integrity, had an adorable boyish grin, but that I didn't think it was going to work out because he lived too far away. Naturally, I would give them more details, but I'd always end by saying, "I really wish he wasn't so precious!" Shortly after I arrived home, Adam called to make sure I had gotten home safely. It's hard to believe we had more to talk about, but we talked for almost another half hour that night.

The next day I started getting texts from him during the day and calls at night. I could've decided not to answer, but for some reason I just couldn't resist him. He began to be more and more endearing to me; and before I knew it, he was coming to my town after church the next Sunday just to spend the day. We had lunch and then started walking around town. I had conveniently arranged for Ann and her husband to be right where we were so they could meet. After all, she was the one who kept telling me to "date the teacher." When we met up with them, we chatted for only a short time and then went on our way to do some more sightseeing. At the end of the day we went to Starbucks where he ordered the largest coffee sold and put tons of sugar packs in it (I found out later that he didn't even drink coffee but agreed to go there because I wanted to. In fact, he said he was wired all night long from drinking it!). We had a hard time saying goodbye. I reminded myself that this was a guy who lived too far away, and both of us had already said that neither of us was willing to move for a relationship.

Adam and I continued talking every night and texting back and forth during the day. We didn't see each other over Christmas because we both had family activities we needed to participate in. In addition, I wasn't sure that the relationship was going to continue, so why would I want to introduce families?

On New Year's Eve one of the Fab Four was having a party, and I thought it would be the perfect time for my other girlfriends to meet Adam, so I invited him. He got a hotel room downtown, which was about twenty minutes from where I lived. We arrived at the party a little late; and after meeting the other people, he headed right for the table where Ann was sitting, and he stayed there for most of the night. He and Ann had a special bond right from the beginning. I understood Ann's part because Adam reminded her of her brother who had passed away a few years prior, but Adam just loved her from the beginning as if she were the "sister he never had."

No other man had ever made me feel as pretty and as cherished as Adam did. He constantly complimented me and told me how he couldn't stop thinking about me. After having experienced so much negativity and loneliness in my life, I was really swept off my feet by him; however, when I went to his hometown and saw the tiny house he lived in (Around 800 square feet), I was less than impressed. He also dressed sloppily, and I was used to and attracted by men who dressed very professionally. There were so many reasons for me to walk away from this relationship, but I got the strongest sense from God that I was where I was supposed to be. During my first visit to his hometown, I met his sons, their wives, and the grandkids, and instantly felt a strong connection to each of them, too. Every time Adam and I parted ways, I would talk to God about the things that were different in our lives and why we weren't a "match," and each time I felt that God was telling me to hang in there.

I shared with the Fab Four how I was feeling about Adam. My head said to stop seeing him, but I felt like God was telling me to stay. I really wanted their input, so after I had dated him for only four months, they arranged a couples' weekend. That way they and their husbands could get to know him better. During that time the group put Adam on the "hot seat" and began grilling him about his intentions with me. I think anybody else would have run, but he handled the questions like a pro. He understood that they were trying to protect me. When I asked him later how that made him feel, he said, "It just convinced me that I wanted to marry you. I don't know when, but it's going to happen." I was almost speechless all the way home. How could he say something like that? We'd only been dating for a short period and all long distance.

Adam had been having some gut pains since we first met. He said they had been going on for a long time and for me not to worry. Suddenly the pains seemed to be getting worse, so I finally insisted that he go to the doctor. After several tests the doctor discovered that Adam had a very large mass on his liver and pancreas. Further testing revealed that he had stage 4 pancreatic and liver cancer; but Adam had a solid faith in God, and he insisted strongly that God was not through with him yet. He firmly believed God had a much higher calling on his life than just being a teacher and former coach. His faith amazed even me, and I think I have a lot of faith.

The doctors decided that he should immediately begin an aggressive chemotherapy regimen. Adam continued his positive attitude. His sons and I, along with friends, began researching frantically. We decided we needed to let the treatments begin locally and then we would have him transferred to a research hospital for a second opinion as soon as possible. Below is an email I sent out to hundreds of friends and family on behalf of Adam:

Your prayers for Adam are already working. He went to the surgeon today to discuss the port that needs to be inserted for the chemotherapy. The surgeon informed him that the soonest it could be done was next Friday. Adam kept pushing for an earlier date, but the doctor insisted that there were no open spots. Finally, Adam said, "Jesus and I are ready to get on with this!" The surgeon looked at him for a moment, then said, "We'll work you in tomorrow."

We know that our God is the same God who breathed the universe into existence. One of the scriptures in our devotion this morning was Luke 12:25 (NASB) – "Who of you by worrying can add a single hour to your life?"

Nobody likes to face any type of hardship, but we all will, at some point in our lives, face at least one "Goliath." Adam's Goliath is now named Cancer. He's getting his slingshot ready to go into battle, holding on to God's hand and leaning on His everlasting arms. A recent sermon Adam heard said: "Don't worry, worship." He has been saying this to me for many weeks and it has become his "battle cry."

We feel peace during what otherwise would be earth-shattering news. The verse that I have always claimed as my "life verse" is Jeremiah 29:11 (NIV) "For I know the plans I have for you" declares the Lord, "plans to prosper you and not to harm you, to give you hope and a future." I now claim this over Adam's life, too.

Cancer is BIG, especially Pancreatic Cancer... BUT our God is even bigger!

Adam's sons took him to the doctor's office to get his port put in, but he was immediately taken to the hospital emergency room because of the rapid growth of his tumors. I was working in North Georgia when I got the call and drove as fast as I could to get there, cutting the four-hour drive down to less than three. The next two days went by quickly. There was a constant line of visitors to his hospital room. We finally had to cut them off because Adam was getting so weak. The second day only his children, step-children, and I were allowed in the room. Naturally, his mother, brother, and other family members came in for short visits; however, the hospital set up a private waiting room where the family visited with the ongoing stream of Adam's visitors. About mid-day the kids were taking turns telling me hilarious stories about him. The room was full of laughter. We knew Adam would love hearing the laughter and feeling the love that was in that room, and during one of those stories, Adam took his last breath on earth. It had only been nine days since his diagnosis.

The Fab Four drove the two and a half hours to be with me the next day. I don't think I could have made it through that time without them; however, Adam's boys and their wonderful wives were so strong, he would have been very proud of them. The funeral was huge because he was such a popular, caring man. In fact, it was the second largest funeral in the capital city's history, according to the funeral home. The outpouring of love blew me away. All three local television stations covered his death and funeral. They called him the "Hometown Hero." Adam had grown up, gone to college, and served as a teacher, coach, athletic director, and city councilman without ever leaving his hometown. And I had friends from all periods of my life who drove the distance to attend the funeral in support of me. Most touching was that my son drove three and a half hours to be with me, too. I think my heart, although broken, grew even bigger that day.

The Fab Four drove me back home after the funeral. I walked into my house and immediately went to bed. I wept harder than I ever had before. The sadness of all the losses in my life came back to visit me, and I couldn't make myself get out of bed for several days. When I finally got up, I drove to Walmart and just walked slowly through the store. I'm not sure why I was there, but I remember feeling as if I was having an out of body experience. I sensed that the whole world was going on, but I wasn't part of it. I then realized what being clinically depressed must feel like, and it's not good! I drove back home and went back to bed.

I was mad at God! I mean, EXTREMELY angry with Him! He knew before I met Adam that his time on this earth was short. I wanted to walk away from the relationship again and again, but God convinced me to stay. He assured me that staying in the relationship with Adam was what I was supposed to do. His friends and family kept telling me that I was "the angel God sent Adam for the last chapter of his life." I said to God, "That's all well and good for Adam, but what about ME?" With everything I had been through in my life, why did God think I was strong enough to go through one more thing? Then I remembered a quote from C.S. Lewis: "Hardship often prepares an ordinary person for an extraordinary destiny." God used that quote to get me out of bed and back to living. He also reminded me that none of this situation was about me. The truth is, I have no clue why God has allowed me to go through so many trials. But I trust Him that He always has had a plan for me.

CHAPTER NINE

You Can't Heal What You Don't Feel

Jesus returned to the Sea of Galilee and climbed a hill and sat down. A vast crowd brought him the lame, blind, crippled, mute, and many others with physical difficulties, and they laid them before Jesus. And he healed them all.
Matthew 15:29-30 (NIV)

When I finally got to the point that I could no longer handle things on my own, no longer stand the pain and shame, I threw myself at the foot of the cross and cried out to God for His intervention and deliverance. I had prayed to Him in the past and had even given the situations of my life over to Him. Momentarily. But for some reason I would always take them back again. This time I was determined to let God have my entire messy life once and for all. I have learned that God can truly mend a broken heart, but you must be willing to give Him ALL the pieces. My pastor, Rev. Michael Fife, once said, "Humpty Dumpty sat on a wall. Humpty Dumpty had a great fall. All the king's horses and all the king's men couldn't put Humpty together again. But God can!"; however, He needs *all* the pieces to do it. You can't hold anything back.

I do not claim to be an expert on anything. I am neither a pastor nor a psychologist, but God has taught me a lot in my path to healing, which is why I believe He led me to put my story down in writing. I needed a way to share it with people like you. The information in this book is not based on anything scientific, nor the result of years of theological study. It is simply things that a mighty, loving, compassionate God revealed to a broken, battered, ordinary woman.

As I said earlier, admitting what had happened all the way back to my childhood and cleaning out the "secret closet" of my heart was the first step in releasing all the pain. There were memories locked in there that my mind had even forgotten. As I would give them back to God, one by one, He took them and did away with them. For good. Corrie Ten Boom said, "God takes our sins – the past, present, and future, and dumps them in the sea and puts up a sign that says No Fishing Allowed." Yes, I still have the experiences in my memory, but they don't *control* me anymore. The best thing is that they don't determine my self-esteem anymore either.

God used a variety of people to help me with my healing: my counselor, my pastor, and a few very close friends. Choosing the right counselor is extremely critical. As a Christian, I didn't want just anyone for this task, so I asked around in the Christian community to find whom pastors most recommended. If Christian counselors aren't available ask them for referrals. Don't just go to anyone. Get references!

One of the most important things to do in recovery is to get an accountability partner (or partners). Finding the right one(s) should also be a matter of much prayer. You need people who are grounded in the Word and who reflect Christ in their everyday lives. The accountability partner also needs to be someone you can be totally honest with, sharing the good and the bad. I was blessed to find a small group of four ladies who fit these criteria, my "Fab Four." One went to church with me and three didn't. In fact, the others are members of three different churches and denominations. We met on a Walk to Emmaus retreat, and after that weekend we began meeting every Monday morning at seven o'clock in the morning, to share, lift each other up, and pray for each other. That was almost twenty-three years ago! Even to this day we each minister to one another. Having them to share with has been a tremendous blessing to me. Not only have my partners kept me from seeing myself as a loser, they also have kept me from throwing myself any more pity parties. These ladies have become closer than sisters. They are my first call when I need prayer and my first call to share good news. We have laughed together, cried together, confronted one another, consoled each other, supported each other, and grown closer to God and each other through this special bond as prayer partners.

There is never any reason to face the trials of life alone. Ask God to show you someone you can have as an accountability partner. You can also ask for your pastor's help in linking you to the right person. Just make sure that the person is the same sex as you and living a godly lifestyle. I know that finding the time to meet with someone can be very difficult, so I'd recommend "Phone a Friend." If you're a stay-at-home mom, use your kid's naptime to call your prayer partner. If you have a hectic job, shut the door to your office at lunch and take that time to phone, email, tweet, or text your friend.

Healing is a series of steps. My healing certainly didn't happen overnight. I heard one time that if you'll take the first step, God will take the second step. By the time you get to the third step, you'll realize that it was God who gave you the strength and courage to take the first step in the first place. That's so true! I think the first step is admitting that you have a problem bigger than you can handle. What you have is a God-sized problem. You need to then humble yourself and ask for God's help. That doesn't mean that He will always take you out of the situation. Sometimes God wants to heal you amid the circumstances.

I believe when I began to cry about all the pain and shame that I stuffed down in my heart, I was allowing myself to feel the pain for the first time. As long as I continued to ignore the problem, I didn't have to feel the pain; however, when we hold on to whatever hurts (pain, shame, low self-esteem, sin, etc.), we are not releasing them so our Heavenly Father can take them away from us. I've come to learn that healing is a gift from God. Much like salvation, it's always there, and it's free. He offers us the ability to be healed and says, "Take it, it's yours." But we must reach out and accept the gift. He won't force it on us. God wants us to be whole. He wants us to be free. He wants us to be His! So often we use God like an emergency kit. We go bumping along in life until we get hurt. Then we take Him out, blow off the dust, and say, "Make the pain go away." That's what I did for too many years. All along God had the miracle cure, but I didn't ask for it. I only asked for Band-Aids to cover the pain. Your Heavenly Father wants you to feel the pain, come to Him, and allow Him to heal you. Completely.

CHAPTER TEN

THE BIG D

"I hate divorce," says the LORD God.
Malachi 2:16 (NLT)

Without a shadow of a doubt, I believe that divorce is against the will of God. Does that sound strange coming from someone who has been divorced three times? (Even putting those words in writing still stings my heart.) I have no intention of debating the rights and wrongs of divorce. God provides scripture that tells us that His perfect will is for couples to stay married, but the Bible also explains that there are specific times when it's all right for a marriage to end.

Had I stayed married the first time, I have no doubt that I would have suffered increased domestic abuse. Yet when I was going through it, I was convinced that I had done something to cause abusive treatment. I now realize that *NOBODY deserves to be abused*! If you are in an abusive relationship, get help! There are plenty of places you can go for assistance. Almost every town has a shelter for battered and abused women and children. Seek help from a pastor, a counselor, Family and Children Services, or the police. Whatever you do, don't let anyone convince you that domestic abuse is justified!

Even though God says in Matthew 19:9 that "marital unfaithfulness" is grounds for divorce, I still struggled with divorcing my second husband. I agonized over the stigma of being divorced a second time and worried about the emotional anxiety my children would suffer. I wanted my children to grow up and have happy marriages that would last forever. I thought at first that just continuing to live in the same house with their daddy would ensure they would have wonderful, committed relationships with their future spouses. After all, I had always heard about couples that "stayed together for the kids"; however, I now realize that kids mirror in their own lives what is patterned in their home. If you want your kids to have a happy, healthy marriage, you need to do whatever it takes to make yours like that, too.

As I stated earlier, I went through several years of counseling to become emotionally well. I believe that you must have two healthy individuals to have a healthy marriage, and I was determined to do my part. I didn't stop with just going to counseling; I have also prioritized reading Christian materials about what a solid marriage consists of. In fact, I now have a personal library with books that I constantly recommend to other people, especially those who are about to get married.

One of the best books I have read about love, whether romantic love, parental love, or any kind of love relationship, is *The Five Love Languages: The Secret to Love that Lasts* by Gary Chapman, who explores the five basic ways people give and receive love: Quality Time, Acts of Service, Physical Touch, Words of Affirmation, and Gifts. The book explains the importance of learning what the other person's love language is and then making the effort to express love the way that person needs to receive it. Although we certainly can have a blend of more than one of these languages, we all have a favorite way we like to receive love. Our natural response is to give love back in our own love language; but if the other person's love language is not the same as ours, he or she ends up not feeling loved. This idea was extremely eye opening to me. I highly recommend *The Five Love Languages* to everyone. (There is even a *Five Love Languages* book written for children and another version for teenagers).

Two other books that I strongly recommend to people are *Marriage on The Rock: God's Design for Your Dream Marriage* by Jimmy Evans, and *Men Are Like Waffles --Women Are Like Spaghetti* by Bill and Pam Farrel. Both books use everyday examples and humor to explore the differences in men and women, offering suggestions on how to understand and celebrate those differences and in doing so strengthen our relationships. As I read and reread each of these books, I find myself laughing hysterically as well as shaking my head as each book describes characteristics of both sexes that I can relate to. These writings help me understand where I fell short in former relationships and give me guidance and realistic expectations for a future relationship.

God has taught me the importance of study as a means of personal healing and growth. If you find yourself in a less than perfect marriage, you need to do more than just complain. You need to take positive steps to improve it. Start with yourself. Do what you can to become a healthy "you." And pray that God will give your spouse the desire to become a healthy "him" or "her." Hopefully you and your spouse will both agree to read and study ways to improve your marriage (whether you are having problems or not) and will consider Christian marriage counseling and/or attend one of the many Christian marriage seminars that are available all around the country. Remember that the only one who has the power to change another person is God, so take care of improving yourself and leave your spouse to God. Whatever else you do, without fail, pray for your spouse, your marriage, and your children. Every day!

God hates divorce. He hates what it does to the individuals. He hates what it does to the children involved. I believe that divorce is a sin. I also believe that any sin is forgivable. And yet I still struggled with believing that God had forgiven me, and in turn I also couldn't forgive myself. I searched the scriptures and read verse after verse about how God will forgive us for our sins – any sin (except blasphemy against the Holy Spirit). I looked for a verse that said God would not forgive anyone for the sin of divorce, but it wasn't there. Instead, I read verses like, "I'll forever wipe the slate clean of their sins" (Hebrews 10:17 MSG). None of the verses said that God would forgive every sin… except divorce. I had to learn to stop beating myself up about my mistakes, accept God's forgiveness, and move on. I once heard that forgiveness is setting a prisoner free and then finding out that the prisoner is you. For a long time, I have been my own captive prisoner. I am the one who allowed shame to control my life, illuminating the imaginary neon signs. I stood at the front of the line and pointed a finger at myself and yelled, "LOSER!" But God has made me see that if He (our mighty God) can forgive us, then we must let go and forgive ourselves, too.

William Arthur Ward said, "Failure is not fatal. Failure should be our teacher, not our undertaker. It should challenge us to new heights of accomplishments, not pull us to new depths of despair. From honest failure can come valuable experience."

CHAPTER ELEVEN

FATHER KNOWS BEST

If you forgive those who sin against you, your heavenly
Father will forgive you. But if you refuse to forgive
others, your Father will not forgive your sins.
Matthew 6:14-15 (NIV)

I have always envied girls who had a loving relationship with their fathers. One of the biggest desires of my heart was to have that, too; however, that's not the way my relationship was with my dad. As a child I did everything to gain his affection. I knew he was capable of that kind of love because I saw him act that way, especially with my younger brother. I wanted so badly to make up for "ruining his life." I excelled in school. I tried to be a dancer, too, but if I messed up at all, he would make fun of me by calling me "Grace." I ran track, but he never saw a meet. No matter what I did, it was never good enough.

After my parents divorced, I saw my dad only a few times over the following six years. He married a woman with four kids, and they became his family. I loved my dad and hated him at the same time. All I ever wanted was for him to love me! I couldn't understand why I was so unlovable. Isn't it interesting that the opinion of one important person can mold a child's self-image? I heard one time that a negative self-esteem is more destructive than alcohol or drugs. Even though my dad was physically abusive, too, the bruises and scars I endured from his words were a lot more damaging than those physical ones that I received on the rest of my body.

When I escaped the rage of my first husband, I left with only the clothes on my back, a car with a broken door, and about ten dollars to my name. In desperation I called my dad and told him what happened. He seemed sympathetic, arranged for me to pick up a ticket for the airline he worked for, and flew me to see him. During those few days my dad hugged me and told me that he loved me. Even though this time would never repeat itself, those words and that moment will forever be etched in my mind.

Before my healing I was not able to understand when a pastor would say that God is your "loving daddy." There was no way I wanted to think of God being anything like my dad. It wasn't until I heard someone say that God is not the *reflection* of your earthly father, but the *perfection* of him, that I began to contemplate the comparison. Today there is no correlation in my mind. My dad was my biological father, and God is my loving Daddy.

After visiting my dad that time, I tried to keep the lines of communication open. I wrote him letters, and a few times I called him at home. Unfortunately, most of the time he was intoxicated, and his nasty side and criticism came out, so I avoided him as much as possible. Building a relationship with him was still important to me, but most of the time he resisted. I prayed, "God, please heal my relationship with my dad." God said, "Forgive him." I said, "But he was so cruel to me." God said, "Tell him you forgive him." I said, "But God, I can't talk about that with him. He'll be mad at me." God said, "Forgive him." As a growing Christian, I knew that I needed to forgive him, but that step was very difficult for me. I wanted to be free from the bondage that these angry feelings had left me with, but the only way I could forgive him was to pull some of the anger out of my heart and process it. The thought of that pain kept me from moving forward with God's instructions.

When Dad was caught drinking on the job, he was forced to enter an alcohol rehabilitation center. At the same time a visiting preacher at church asked everyone in the congregation to think of a person they needed to forgive. Of course, mine was my dad. The minister instructed us to write a letter to that person to let him/her know that we were offering forgiveness. I decided it was time to confront the demon. I sat down and wrote my dad a long letter. The pastor told us to begin the letter by thanking that person for something they had done and then to tell how they had hurt us, ending with the fact that we were forgiving them and that we loved them. My letter took a long time to write. After mailing it, I began praying that God would use my heartfelt words to heal my relationship with my father.

This exercise gave me such an emotional release. I called about a week later and asked if he had received the letter. He said, "Yes." Then silence. I said, "Dad, I love you." Silence again. It wasn't the reaction I had hoped for, but at least I had been obedient and offered the forgiveness. I've learned that the results are not up to us. When God tells us do something, we are to be obedient. The outcomes are out of our hands. We just have the peace of knowing that we have done the right thing.

Over the next three years I still tried my best to gain my dad's love. He died without my desire being fulfilled. I still feel sadness that I did not succeed in this area, but I also have the peace of knowing that I did everything in my power to reach out and restore the relationship before he died.

Today I allow God to be my father. When I have a bad day, when I'm scared, when I'm sad, or when I want comfort for any reason, I call out to my daddy, God, and imagine myself crawling up in His lap. I can almost feel His strong, loving arms wrapping me in a tight embrace, as He whispers in my ear, "Everything's going to be all right." No pain, no shame, just unmatchable love.

CHAPTER TWELVE

TAKE THE PLUNGE

*I am the vine; you are the branches. If you remain in me and I in
you, you will bear much fruit; apart from me you can do nothing.*
Matthew 15:5 (NIV)

On a Sunday afternoon drive through the country, I turned on
the radio and listened to the end of a sermon where the pastor
(name unknown to me) said that the Christian life is like putting
a tea bag in hot water. If you just dip it a few times, you'll get very
weak tea. But if you let the tea bag *abide* in the water, it becomes
very rich tea, and if you allow the bag to abide in the water
long enough, soon the water and the tea become one. When
compared to our relationship with God, it's easy to see that the
longer we stay in the Word (the Bible), the closer we will come
to God. This simple little analogy hit me hard. Unfortunately, I
was a little dipper for many years. No wonder Satan easily found
people and situations to tear me down and make me feel like one
big hot mess.

When I finally began concentrating on growing in Christ,
God unveiled my eyes to show me that I was not the loser I
had believed myself to be. Even though I have relationships and
decisions in my past that I regret, God has shown me that He has

used all the events of my life, positive and negative, to form the person I am today. "And we know that God causes everything to work together for the good of those who love God and are called according to his purpose for them" (Romans 8:28 NLT). I had to get to the point that I could no longer control things on my own before I allowed God to completely take over.

Now I purposely make choices that will enhance my relationship with God. I surround myself with Christian people who will keep me grounded and focused. I've learned that labeling a person at an early age is like receiving an unfair sentence; it's hard to overcome. Most of the time we become who people say we are. To comfort ourselves, we choose people who are like us to be our friends. To make matters worse, we reject the love and concern of people who would otherwise be healthy for us because we don't think we're good enough for them. The most important person to surround ourselves with is God. If we hold onto His hand, we may stumble, but we will not fall.

In an effort to stay grounded and focused, I try to have a daily quiet time. I use the word *try* because I am not always successful; however, one of the tasks of my accountability partners (the Fab Four) is to ask me if I am having my daily quiet time. This area is where the accountability really pays off. I hate to have to admit when I have slipped up! In addition, I can tell in my own attitude when I miss more than a couple of days. The more I *abide* in the Word and the desire to grow in Christ, the easier it is to stay on task. After several years of personal growth, my daily "quiet time" has expanded. Not only do I read a devotional (or two), I also keep my radio in the car and at work tuned to a Christian station. The more I surround myself with Christian influence, the easier it is to keep a positive attitude and stay focused on my goal of "abiding in Christ."

The first and hardest step in starting a daily quiet time is getting out of bed. I once heard someone say it was "Mind over mattress!" Of course, some people prefer having a nighttime quiet time, and some choose other times during the day. The time of day is not what's important. Everyone should just pick the time that works best for them. Then find a book, grab a Bible, and as my pastor Rev. Fife says, "It's Nike theology...Just do it!"

Reading your Bible is also extremely important and the one thing I personally have struggled with the most. The easiest thing for me to do is to find a personal Bible study. I look for ones that are short but require you to look up different verses. I wish I could say that I can quote you scriptures with the best of them, but then I'd have to ask for forgiveness for lying. Memorization is definitely not one of my spiritual gifts, but I still do my best. I was taught that if you don't know where to start reading in the Bible then start reading one Psalm and one Proverb a day. By the time you're through, the habit will already be established, and then you can let God direct you from there.

Of course, we must do more than just have a quiet time, read our Bibles, and go to church. We must also allow the Word to make a difference in our daily lives. Someone once said, "Reading the Word and not putting it to use in your daily life is like going to the doctor and getting him to write you a prescription. Unless you get the prescription filled and take the medicine, you won't get better."

Since I stopped being a "little dipper" and started abiding in Christ, my life and my attitude about myself have changed immeasurably. A friend of mine always says that when you prayerfully and purposely surround yourself with God, He possesses you. Nothing touches you that hasn't come through Him first. I want to be totally and completely surrounded by God. Don't you? Don't be a dipper...take the plunge!

CHAPTER THIRTEEN

DEVELOP AN ATTITUDE OF GRATITUDE

Be joyful always; pray continually; give thanks in all circumstances, for this is God's will for you in Christ Jesus.
1 Thessalonians 5:16-18 (NIV)

In her book *Boomerang Joy* Barbara Johnson wrote, "We cannot protect ourselves from trouble, but we can dance through the puddles of life with a rainbow smile, twirling the only umbrella we need – the umbrella of God's love. His covering of grace is sufficient for any problem we may have." Yes, problems are inevitable, no matter how tight your walk with the Lord is. In fact, many biblical scholars will tell you that the closer you walk with God the stronger the enemy will attack. Rev. Michael Fife always says, "If you're not running into him (Satan) you're running in the wrong direction"; therefore, we need to develop a good attitude, put on the full armor of God (found in Ephesians 10:6-17), and move forward.

Did I say having a good attitude was easy? Not at all! You always must be on your guard. 1 Peter 5:8 (NLT) says, "Be careful!

Watch out for attacks from the Devil, your great enemy. He prowls around like a roaring lion, looking for some victim to devour." Praise God that He is stronger than any enemy!

After my second husband and I divorced, I was filled with sadness, thoughts of shame and failure, and feelings of being a world-class loser. That imaginary neon sign was shining brighter than ever! The scripture "Be thankful in all circumstances" (1 Thessalonians 5:18 NLT) kept running through my head. Surely God didn't mean that I should be thankful that my twenty-year marriage ended in divorce or that now my children should be grateful that they came from a broken home. How could God expect me to give thanks for those things? I twisted, turned, questioned, cried, and really struggled with this thought. I tried to fake an upbeat attitude, but God knew I wasn't being honest. I really wasn't thankful about the situation at all. When I heard stories about God working miracles in other marriages, I was consumed with jealousy and further allowed Satan to attack through my feelings of unworthiness because God did not answer my prayers to heal my marriage.

Finally, God woke me up in the wee hours one morning. He was not angry with me. Instead, I felt Him wrap His arms around me as He began speaking in a whisper, as a tender loving daddy would talk to his small child. I could envision a smile on His face as He spoke. In His quiet, gentle way He reminded me that if I had not had problems in my marriage, I would never have visited my new church. Had I not visited there, I would not have met and made friends with the wonderful members of the Body of Christ there. God continued to remind me how these people had ministered to my children and me during this time and how my personal growth in Christ had reached a new level. As I continued to imagine myself in the Father's arms, I began to reflect on all the wonderful people that had been added to my life over the period of time I had been separated from my husband. I was overwhelmed with the realization of how blessed I had been!

One by one God brought the faces of my new friends to my mind so I could give thanks for them individually. By the time I fell back asleep my heart was bursting with thankfulness!

I realized that God understood the reason for my broken heart and shattered dreams. He didn't expect me to go through that trial and not hurt. I don't have to give thanks that my marriage ended, but I do give thanks that when I went through that painful time in my life, I had much to be thankful for.

If you look at the scripture at the beginning of this chapter closely, you'll see that the Bible says to be thankful *in* everything not *for* everything. What trials are you facing or have you faced that have left you feeling angry, sad, or discouraged? Go back and ask God to show you how to be thankful *in* your situation. You'll be amazed how finding appreciation for even small things will change your attitude.

It's been said that pain is inevitable, but misery is a choice. Attitude is everything! Ask God to help you to develop an attitude of gratitude.

CHAPTER FOURTEEN

THAT WAS A GOOFY THING TO SAY

Don't worry about anything; instead, pray about everything.
Tell God what you need and thank him for all he has done.
Then you will experience God's peace, which exceeds
anything we can understand. His peace will guard
your hearts and minds as you live in Christ Jesus.
Philippians 4:6-7 (NLT)

Have you ever felt stupid when you prayed out loud when other people could hear? Having been a perfectionist most of my life, I refrained from praying in public for years for fear that people would criticize the way I prayed. Several years ago God delivered me (at least mostly) from being the extreme perfectionist that I always was. My daughter was taking tennis lessons, and her coach decided to give me one free lesson, too. I was horrible! After hitting several "home runs" and tripping over a crack in the pavement, he gave up on me! Upon recounting the story to a friend, I made the mistake of saying that I felt like the cartoon character Goofy. Well, lo and behold, that nickname stuck with me. Today I have a huge collection of Goofy items, coffee cups, nightshirts, hats, Christmas ornaments, etc., that my friends have lovingly given to me. The best thing about the whole "Goofy" nickname is that I learned to stop taking myself so seriously. Now when I mess up, instead of being furious with myself for being less than perfect, I can laugh at myself and say, "Well, after all, I am Goofy."

This attitude has also helped me in my prayer life. I used to think that I had to have this wonderful "prayer language." You know, quoting scripture and words most people would have to look up in the dictionary. Then the more I studied the Word, the more I realized that God isn't concerned about the words we use; He just wants us to talk to Him. If He cared about us using big, fancy words, then why would He tell us that we should come to Him like little children? In Matthew 18:4 (NIV) Jesus said, "I tell you the truth, unless you change and become like little children, you will never enter the kingdom of heaven."

These days I just pray to God the same way I talk to any of my other friends. In fact, sometimes when I pray out loud in a group, I even get tickled and laugh with God, which usually makes the other people laugh, too. I don't worry because I know God has a sense of humor...He's been laughing with me for years!

Don't get me wrong; I can still be in a group and feel very intimidated by some of the more elegant pray-ers in the group, especially when I am with a group of pastors. On one such occasion I was in a small room praying for a friend who was about to give her testimony publicly for the first time. As we were taking turns praying, the two other non-clergy people went first. Both spoke eloquently. Then the three pastors jumped in with their prayers. While the third one was praying, Satan was tapping me on the shoulder saying, "You know you are really going to sound stupid following all these Godly people. You're standing near the door. Run!" I thought about it for a moment, but before I could move, it was my turn. I swallowed hard and went for it. I spoke to God in my very simple, matter of fact way. No scripture, no big words…just me talking to God. After the group broke up, one of the pastors came up to me and said, "I love to hear you pray. I could listen to that all day." I was both shocked and humbled, but mostly I felt affirmed in my belief that it's not the words you use that counts. God just wants to hear what's in your heart.

There are also no rules about where or when you pray. I pray anywhere and anytime. When the alarm goes off in the morning and I'm still lying in my bed, I pray "Good morning, God. Please be with me today every step I take, every decision I make." Years ago when I was caught between the horrible situation at work and the turmoil at home, I began praying every morning when I got in my car, begging God to intervene in both situations. Sometimes praying in my head just wasn't good enough; I needed to speak out loud. So in order that I didn't look like a complete idiot riding down the street talking to myself, I would put my cell phone up to my ear and pray into the phone. When things at work got too tough, I would go into the ladies' room and bury my head in my hands and pray fervently. Do you think God cared that I was lying in the bed, riding in the car, or sitting on the potty? No! He was happy that I was coming to Him with my needs. The time and the place are totally insignificant. In fact, the Bible tells us to "Pray continually" (1 Thessalonians 5:17 NIV), which must mean to pray in any and all places at any and all times.

These days I still pray before I get out of the bed in the morning and on my way to work each day. In fact, I try to always remember to turn the radio off in the car the night before, so when I start the car the next morning the radio doesn't come on. I've learned that if I hear even a few bars of a song or a few words from a news report, Satan uses those to distract me and keep me from concentrating on my prayers. The devil is such a pest!

So don't worry about how you sound or where you are or even what time of day it is. We need to communicate with God – our Best Friend and loving Daddy. Tell Him how much you love Him and how wonderful you think He is. Tell Him you're sorry for any way you have messed up (sinned) and ask for His forgiveness. Thank Him for all that He has done for you and those you know and love. And then pray for yourself and others.

Unfortunately, Satan may tap you on the shoulder from time to time offering discouragement and excuses why you shouldn't pray. But don't listen to him! Remember that he is the one who wants you to believe you're a loser. God says you are a winner! So, keep your head up and your knees down!

CHAPTER FIFTEEN
PASS THE SALT, PLEASE!

*You are the salt of the earth. But if the salt loses its saltiness,
how can it be made salty again? It is no longer good for
anything, except to be thrown out and trampled by men.*
Matthew 5:13 (NIV)

Driving through the rural countryside of middle Georgia one day while contemplating why God wanted me to write a book, I happened to turn on the radio. As usual, I scanned the airwaves for a Christian station. I finally landed on one that was in the middle of a sermon. I didn't fully understand the pastor's name, but I listened intently to what he was saying: "We are the salt of the world, but God doesn't call us to stay in the salt shaker. The world is crying out, 'Pass the salt!' We need to get out of our comfortable salt shaker and go season the world." God used this message to say to me, "See, that's what I'm trying to get you to do. I have helped you become very salty, and now you need to pass the salt."

Writing this book was extremely emotional for me; for that reason I was very thankful that the lady who owned the rental cabin offered me the opportunity to get away by myself to accomplish this task. God knew that the trip down memory lane would not be an easy journey. On one hand, it has been humbling to put my life story down in writing. At times Satan came tapping me on the shoulder trying to force me to revisit my feelings of being a hot mess loser. He held the neon sign before me and said, "This belongs to you." Praise God, I had the guts to share with the Fab Four and a few other prayer partners that God had directed me to write and asked that they cover me with prayer while I was away. I most definitely have felt their prayers during my writing. Before beginning I told God that I still wasn't sure why He needed me to write my life story but asked Him to anoint my words and guide my mind and my hands, which I pray He has done.

To be honest, I'm still not sure for whom I have really written. Through this process God has reminded me several times that you can't give to others what you don't have yourself. There are no words to express the level of gratitude I have for God plucking me out of my loser mentality and placing my feet upon the solid rock of Jesus Christ. I have learned that God sees us as His precious children and He loves us very, very much. Picture for a moment the person on this earth you think loves you the most. Now think how great his or her love is for you. I can assure you that by comparison, that person's love is a teardrop compared to the ocean of God's love! To put the idea another way, I once heard someone say that God's love is like trying to take a drink from a fire hydrant...it's so grand, it will blow you away!

So how do you feel about yourself? Are you a winner or a loser? Have you faced trials that have seemed too hard or have left you feeling like a failure? Give them over to God. He will take all your trials and turn them into triumphs. It's never too late. Remember that God loves you just the way you are, but He also loves you too much to let you stay that way.

This is a simple book with a simple message of the love and grace offered by our Lord Jesus Christ. He wants us to be healthy. He wants us to be whole. He wants us to know that we are loved. And when we get to the point that we can accept all these gifts for ourselves...then He wants us to "Pass the Salt!"

CHAPTER SIXTEEN

Is That Your Final Answer?

Therefore, there is now no condemnation for
those who are living in Christ Jesus.
Romans 8:1 (NIV)

Unfortunately, Satan loves to throw "the bad stuff" back in our faces to bring us down and put a wedge between God and us. He knows our weaknesses. One of mine is poor self-esteem. Though God has done a fantastic job in my healing, there are times when Satan sneaks "zingers" in on me. For instance, when I changed churches after my husband and I separated, I didn't tell people why. I had shared the situation with the pastor and only a few close friends, but I asked them to keep it quiet. Why? First, it was nobody's business, and I was hoping my husband and I would end up getting back together after we worked things out through counseling. Secondly, my children had grown up in that church, and I didn't want them to be embarrassed. What I hadn't counted on was that when people don't know the truth, they make it up. One of my dear friends from that church would occasionally tell me the latest rumor about me: Once someone said I was the one who had an affair; another time, I was babysitting for a couple from my new church, and when someone saw me at the mall with their baby, the rumor became not only did I have an affair, I now also had a baby! I even heard that I was having a nervous breakdown because of my recent hysterectomy.

I'd be lying if I said these attacks didn't bother me. I'm hurt that my "friends" would believe lies about me so easily. I regret that the truth can never be revealed about the sexual harassment from work. When I see other families together, especially during the holidays, I'm deeply saddened that my kids must deal with the complications of a broken family. Yes, these things hurt my heart...BUT...they no longer control me. When those painful moments happen, I immediately take them to God. If I need earthly support, I go immediately to my husband, my (now adult) children and my accountability partners, the Fab Four. I do my best not to harbor any anger or unforgiveness in my heart because I have learned that not only are those feelings against God's desire for us, if we do hold on to that junk, we only hurt *ourselves.*

So how can you guard yourself from Satan's attacks?

- As soon as you realize you are under attack, PRAY and ask for God's intervention and strength.
- Find scriptures that encourage you. Write them on postcards or sticky notes and display them around your house, put them in your glove compartment or console, stick a few in your desk drawer, purse, or wallet.
- Listen to Christian music with lyrics that remind you of the love, grace and forgiveness of Christ.
- Find an accountability partner or partners who will lift you up, dare to confront you when you seem to be falling back into old habits, and remind you *Whose* you are.
- Make a conscious effort to reprimand Satan as soon as you realize you're under attack by saying something like

"Get behind me Satan. I'm covered by the blood of Jesus."
Be sure to speak with power.

- Read Christian books that directly address the struggles
you are facing or books that address your weaknesses.
Because I have not been successful in relationships of
the heart, not only have I read books about marriage (as
mentioned in Chapter 7), I also read books on how to find
the right person God has for you. One of the best books I
have read on this topic is *Date or Soul Mate? How To Tell
If Someone Is Worth Pursuing In Two Dates Or Less* by Neil
Clark Warren, PhD.

Going through any storm in your life is never easy. At one of
my darkest times, when my twenty-year marriage was ending
and I was also dealing with the sexual harassment issue at work,
I was so beaten down that I actually asked God to let me die!
That's how depressed I had become. Death seemed like a better
option than what I was experiencing at the time. But today, after
allowing God to heal me, I can honestly say that I see a purpose
for everything I have gone through because it has brought me
into the relationship I now have with God. When I found myself
up against a wall with nowhere to turn, God was able to show
His power, grace, and mercy in ways that my children and I
would never have experienced otherwise.

In his book *The Purpose Driven Life: What On Earth Am I
Here For?* Rick Warren writes, "You are not an accident. Your
birth was no mistake or mishap, and your life is no fluke of
nature. Your parents may not have planned you, but God did.
He was not at all surprised by your birth. In fact, he expected it."
When I read these words, I felt like God had written them just
for me. I spent most of my life focusing on my dad's words, "You
were a mistake. You should never have been born" instead of my
Heavenly Daddy's words, "I am your Creator. You were in my care

even before you were born" (Isaiah 44:2 CEV). I spent years in bondage to the loser sign, but by the grace of God, I am now free!

I conclude this chapter with an excerpt from one of my favorite authors, Max Lucado. These words have encouraged me. May they do the same for you.

> "Every moment of your life, your accuser is filing charges against you. He has noticed every error and marked every slip...Try to forget your past; he'll remind you. Try to undo your mistakes; he will thwart you.
>
> This expert witness has no higher goal than to take you to court and press charges.
>
> Who is he?
>
> The devil...
>
> He rails: "This one you call your child, God. He is not worthy..."
>
> As he speaks, you hang your head. You have no defense. His charges are fair.
>
> "I plead guilty, your honor," you mumble.
>
> "The sentence?" Satan asks.
>
> "The wages of sin is death," explains the judge, "but in this case the death has already occurred. For this one died with Christ."
>
> Satan is suddenly silent. And you are suddenly jubilant...
>
> You have stood before the judge and heard him declare, "Not guilty."
>
> (from *In The Grip Of Grace*)

CHAPTER SEVENTEEN

MY HAPPILY EVER AFTER

*"Be strong. Take courage. Don't be intimidated. Don't
give them a second thought because GOD, your God,
is striding ahead of you. He's right there with you.
He won't let you down; he won't leave you."*
Deuteronomy 31:6 (MSG)

After Adam passed away, I was 100% done with pursuing a romantic relationship. I was finally content being single for the rest of my life. God had blessed me with two great kids, fabulous friends, and two adorable grandsons. My life was very full without a man.

Throughout my adult life I remained friends with Amy (the friend who was instrumental in introducing me to Jesus and who convinced me to go to college with her). She had married her high school boyfriend, Jerry, and I saw them as often as possible when I was visiting the Atlanta area. Amy kept encouraging me to date Jerry's best friend Neil, whom I had known since middle school. But he was always "just a friend" to me. He had even come with Jerry to visit us at college, and Amy and I would fix him up with our girlfriends. Even if I had been interested, I was usually dating someone else whenever he wasn't dating anyone.

Neil did marry once, but the marriage ended after five years. He also had a career that kept him in Atlanta and I had no desire to move back to that area. Over the years Neil and I saw each other at class reunions, weddings, and funerals and always sat together because we both wanted to sit with Amy and Jerry. Naturally, being at these events alone and having gone through similar disappointments gave us a lot to chat about; however, we never communicated in-between our chance meetings.

A little over a year after Adam passed away, I attended the wedding of Amy and Jerry's son. I arrived a little late, so I slipped into the first open seat I found. When I got to the reception, I stood around looking for someone I knew. Suddenly I heard a voice from behind say, "Well, hello!" I turned around to find Neil standing there, only this time I got butterflies in my stomach, something that had never happened to me before. I thought to myself, "Why am I feeling this way? This is just Neil." I gave him a quick hug and asked him if he wanted to sit with me. He pulled out the chair and sat down. The table filled up quickly with other people we knew, but I found myself just wanting to talk to Neil. I had intended to stay at the reception for only a short time, but now I found myself having a hard time leaving even though the friend I was staying with was waiting for me to return to her home so we could go to a movie together. Finally, I had to go. I knew I would see Neil very soon because, unfortunately, Amy's daddy's funeral was the following day.

I arrived early at the church for that service. Amy's parents had been so special to me when I was a hurting teenager, so this was a very emotional time for me, too; nonetheless, I also found myself looking for Neil. I took a seat in a pew toward the front of the church and left just enough room for another person to sit beside me. As the church was filling up, Neil came in and asked if anyone was sitting in that vacant spot. Naturally I said "No" and invited him to sit down. After the funeral everyone went to Amy's home, including Neil and me. I was engaged in conversation with others but was constantly looking for Neil. He was nowhere to be found.

Finally, it was time for me to leave for the long drive back home. I walked through the entire house to tell everyone goodbye and give hugs to all the friends and family, but I still didn't see Neil anywhere. Amy walked me outside to say goodbye, and I finally saw Neil and Jerry standing in the front yard. Neil immediately stopped talking and said he'd walk me to my car. On the way he suggested that because I came to Atlanta regularly for work, we should get together for dinner sometime. On the ride back home I kept wondering if he was talking about getting together as friends or perhaps he was asking me out on a date. The next day at work, as I was planning out my work visits for the week, I conveniently figured out how I could "just happen" to be back in Neil's area. I sent him an email and said, "If it's not too soon...." He responded by affirming that it wasn't too soon because he had wanted to date me since high school. That made me smile really big!

I decided the time had come to give dating Neil a chance. At the beginning of our first date, we shook hands and agreed that we had to stay friends even if dating didn't work out for us. After all, we had lots of mutual friends, and we would most likely be running into each other for the rest of our lives, even if randomly. The most wonderful thing about Neil is that I had confided in him through the years; therefore, he knew about my other relationships, but he never looked at me as broken, a failure, or a loser. Because of all I had been through, my friends and I really put him through the dating wringer. You might have thought he was under surveillance or part of an FBI investigation. I'm happy to say that he passed all the "tests" with flying colors. Sixteen months after we started dating, with the approval of the Fab Four and my children, we were married. This time I listened. To my closest friends. To my kids. To my God.

We've now been married for almost four years. I continue to thank God every day for Neil. And I'm thrilled to say that I finally found my happily ever after!

CHAPTER EIGHTEEN

LESSONS LEARNED FROM A HOT MESS LIFE

For I know the plans I have for you," declares the LORD, "plans to prosper you and not to harm you, plans to give you hope and a future.
Jeremiah 29:11 (NIV)

God has taught me a lot. A great deal of emotional pain came with some of those lessons. I hated them while I was living them out. I endured embarrassment. Humiliation. Shame. I felt lost. Abandoned. Unloved. I questioned God. Was angry at God. Pushed God away. But in the end I accepted forgiveness from God. Trusted Him. Loved Him. Invited Him to rule my life.

What did I learn from a long life of hills and valleys? I learned that we can't control other people. We can't control their actions or their decisions. We can't control their tongues when they talk about us. When they point fingers at us. We can't control their attitudes. Their opinions. Their critical words.

I've learned that my self-esteem, who I am and what I've done, isn't based on anyone else's list of rights and wrongs. It's only based on who Jesus is and my relationship with Him. I don't need to seek forgiveness from anyone except those whom I've wronged, myself, and Jesus. And without a doubt, one of the most meaningful things to do is to forgive those who have hurt us, regardless of the circumstances. If we don't, we are the ones who suffer as emotional hostages, not them.

I've learned that even though my list of mistakes, failures, and screw-ups is long, Jesus has wiped them all away...because I asked him to. And the fact that I remember them doesn't mean He hasn't forgiven me. There are still consequences. Sometimes remembering keeps me from repeating my mistakes. And I've learned that God can use our messes and mistakes to help others when they are going through something similar. The most important lesson to remember is that God ALWAYS forgives when we ask.

I've learned that sometimes we are our own worst enemy. We are consumed by false guilt. We let ourselves be imprisoned by shame. We are the first to stand in line and criticize ourselves. We look at others and imagine what they are thinking and saying about us with their wagging tongues. Sometimes we're right, but often we are wrong.

I've learned a lot about friendships. True friends. I have learned who they are and how important they are. I have found them to be my chosen family. My "Jesus kin." I have learned the importance of being that kind of friend to other people.

I've learned about prayer, the need to pray. For ourselves and for others. And the need to humble ourselves and ask others to pray for us. I have learned the POWER in prayer and the need to listen to God when He speaks to us or when He points us in a new direction. I have learned the importance of refusing to twist what He's saying to match what I want to hear.

I've learned that instead of picking up the pile of imaginary neon signs saying what a loser I am...What a failure I am...What a hot mess I am...I need to embrace what God says about me. It's a hard thing to do on your own. That's a big reason we need Jesus to be our constant companion.

I am just an ordinary woman who has learned to trust. Follow. Love. And worship an extraordinary God. These days people are always commenting on my smile. They don't see the pain. They don't see the disgrace. They don't see the neon signs. God has taken them all away. He has pulled me up from the deep, dark pit where I saw myself as a loser and believed that the world saw me that way, too. When I feel like I am sliding back down in that pit, I reach out to Him and He pulls me up into His pit. His armpit. As He wraps His arms around me and draws me into a tight embrace of His unconditional love. He has rescued my "loser" mentality and replaced it with His own. And it's His heart's desire to do the same for you!

How does this story end? The truth is that I'm not sure. My story isn't over yet, but I'm excited to live out the rest of my days with Jesus by my side. Recently I saw a sign and had to buy it for our home. It reads, "It's a Wonderful Life"; and indeed, it is.

Let God Have the Final Word -
He Says I'm Not A Loser,
And neither are you!

THANK YOU, GOD!

You turned my wailing into dancing;
You removed my sackcloth and clothed me with joy,
that my heart may sing to you and not be silent.
O Lord my God, I will give you thanks forever.
Psalm 30:11-12 (NIV)

You did it; you changed wild lament into whirling dance;
You ripped off my black mourning band
I'm about to burst with song;
I can't keep quiet about you.
God, my God,
I can't thank you enough!
Psalm 30:11-12 (MSG)

Works Cited

Chapman, Gary. *The Five Love Languages: The Secret to Love that Lasts*. Chicago: Northfield Publishing, 1992.

Evans, Jimmy. *Marriage On The Rock: God's Design For Your Dream Marriage*. Grand Rapids: Zondervan Publishing House, 1994.

Farrel, Bill and Pam Farrel. *Men Are Like Waffles --Women Are Like Spaghetti*. Eugene: Harvest House Publishers, 2001.

"Hot Mess." *UrbanDictionary.com*. <https://www.urbandictionary.com/define.php?term=hot%20mess>.

Johnson, Barbara. *Boomerang Joy*. Grand Rapids: Zondervan Publishing House, 1998.

Lewis, C.S. <https://www.azquotes.com/quote/434691>.

Lucado, Max. *A Gentle Thunder*. Nashville: W Publishing Group, 1995.

Lucado, Max. *In The Grip Of Grace*. Dallas: Word Publishing, 1996. <https://www.smileofachild.org/resources/index.php/2/2018/179.html>.

Myers, G.A. and LeeAnn Weiss. *Hugs from Heaven: The Christmas Story*. Dallas: Simon and Schuster, 1999.

Ram, Buck. *Oh Yes, I'm the Great Pretender*. New York: Peermusic Publishing, 1956.

Smalley, Gary and John Trent, PhD. *The Gift of the Blessing*. Nashville: Thomas Nelson Publishers, 1993.

Ten Boom, Corrie. *Tramp For the Lord*. Nashville: G.P. Putnam's Sons, 1971.

Ward, William Arthur. <u><https://www.azquotes.com/quote/602973></u>.

Warren, Neil Clark. *Date or Soul Mate? How To Tell If Someone Is Worth Pursuing In Two Dates Or Less*. Nashville: Thomas Nelson, Inc., 2002.

Warren, Rick. *The Purpose Driven Life*. Grand Rapids: Zondervan, 2002.

Printed in the United States
By Bookmasters